Billy is a remark ||||||||||||||||| ... adversity and
has become a stro ... God. His touching story of re-
demption shows the unwavering love of our God, and will
captivate and inspire many readers to not only emulate Billy
but, more importantly, God.

—Lorne Korol
Chaplain, Winnipeg Blue Bombers
Winnipeg Jets, Manitoba Moose

As a pastor for the last twenty years, I have walked with many
different people who, like Billy, have also found themselves
in desperate need of a personal breakthrough. My eyes have
seen turning points where great things have sprung out of the
ashes of broken lives. This book casts a glowing light on the
reality that, with the true living God, our very darkest valleys
can become our greenest gardens. It made me feel like it's
never too late to change course from a destructive path to a
constructive one. Even the most down-and-out victims can
experience the power to change into heroes going forward.

Billy, I'm proud to know you. Your life has positively im-
pacted me, your family, and many strangers along the way. I
am certain your readers will be blessed!

—George Balaktsis
Bachelor of Human Ecology, Family Studies
Pastor, West End Christian Community
Winnipeg, MB

Billy enjoys food. Even as a child, he was eager for his mother to teach him how to concoct delicious foods that serve up comfort to Greek families. Billy tried his own recipes, but realized a large amount of cinnamon does not enhance pizza sauce.

That failure pales in comparison to Billy's early life recipe—cultural clashes, parental expectations, bullying from neighborhood kids, alcohol and drug abuse, failed romance and rejection from family left him with a bad taste in his mouth.

Billy found a better recipe, even though he had to endure burning issues along the way. He realizes his story may help others avoid the consequences of a bad mix.

I first met Billy when he was still serving up pizza in a small shop in Winnipeg. Later, we sat down to talk about putting his life story into print. I am pleased he has persisted, and that you can now learn why he chooses to follow the fire.

—Pat Gerbrandt
freelance writer/editor
former columnist for *Christian Week*

Following the Fire

the

A True Story of Conquering Addiction and Overcoming Suicidal Thoughts

Bill Vassilopoulos

FOLLOWING THE FIRE
Copyright © 2017 by Bill Vassilopoulos

ISBN: 978-1-4866-1545-2

Word Alive Press
131 Cordite Road, Winnipeg, MB R3W 1S1
www.wordalivepress.ca

WORD ALIVE
—P R E S S—

Cataloguing in Publication may be obtained through Library and Archives Canada

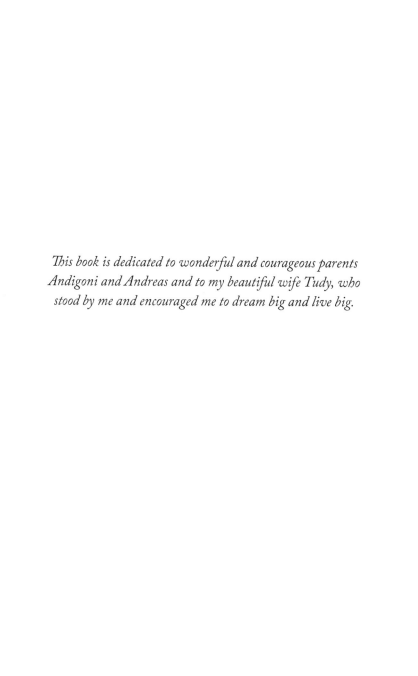

This book is dedicated to wonderful and courageous parents Andigoni and Andreas and to my beautiful wife Tudy, who stood by me and encouraged me to dream big and live big.

content

Acknowledgements

Thank you, Pat Gerbrandt, for taking on the daunting task of doing the first edit to my very rough draft of Following the Fire. Your time and effort is beyond appreciated. Thanks for being a dear friend.

Thank you also to Clint Toews for not giving up on me. I know that I didn't make it easy for you in the beginning but you stuck it out. The world needs more men like you mentoring our young troubled men. Keep up the good work!

Thank you, Pastor George, for picking up the phone back in 2001, and meeting with me. Your passion and love for Jesus was and is contagious. It has really rubbed off on me. Let us never stop following the fire that Jesus has put in our hearts.

Foreword

Anyone who reads this amazing real-life drama might easily believe that the story it tells has been fictionalized. I am here to say that I know Billy well; I know many of the characters mentioned; and I know Billy's story to be true.

This is the deeply moving account of a sensitive, creative and fun-loving son of immigrant parents. A boy who lost his way in life, Billy entered the chaotic and dangerous world of drug dealing, violent confrontation, prison and family conflict. The reader will want to stand up and cheer when reading of his encounters with the love of God who drew him from the edge of suicide into the circle of restoration, standing on a new foundation of confident faith and loving relationships. The turbulence of his past life has been replaced by a peace that surpasses logic. Billy has expressed his deep gratitude many times for the unconditional love of God which defeated the dark forces invading his life and guided him to a life of faith and fullness.

After being a mentor to Billy for fifteen years, I continue to be amazed at the man he has become: a man who is a devoted father to his children, a loving husband, and a man who invests his life daily in the care of those who struggle with life's circumstances. His prayer and mine is that his story will bring hope to the hopeless, courage to the defeated, healing to the brokenhearted and renewed faith to the faltering.

—Clint Toews
Author, Family Counsellor

chapter one

Home, Secure
Home

My name is Billy but when I was born in February 1970, I was named Vasilios Vassilopoulos. It was a fitting name for the first son of a very traditional Greek family. The English translation of our Greek name—Vassilopoulos— is "Son of the King," and my first name, Vasilios, similarly means "kingly one," but something impressive gets lost in translation, and my name comes out as Bill or Billy.

Although they lived in Winnipeg when I was born, both of my parents were determined our home would maintain the Greek traditions that meant so much to them. According to my father, there is no place more beautiful than Greece, and for him, keeping tradition is part of honoring the beauty of his heritage.

When I was young, I didn't care much about those traditions. I only knew that Dad was often absent from home. He worked twelve hours a day at a meat-packing job where they called him "Zorbas." My dad always chose to see the good in others, so he trusted his coworkers and thought it was a cool nickname. When I was a little older and realized what they meant by the nickname, I didn't have the heart to tell him that his coworkers and supervisors were making fun of him. Maybe he did understand at least a little, and maybe that's why he called me by the English form of Vasilios, Billy.

My first awareness of God came when I was around eight years old. I dreamed that my mother and I were sitting at the front of the sanctuary in a Greek church like the one our family attended. A heavily bearded man in a black robe, swinging a lit censer with incense, walked down the center aisle. The congregation members crossed themselves while they bowed in prayer. Smoke from the censer filled the room, rising to obscure the chandeliers.

Then fear gripped me as I sensed that my mother was no longer with me. When the smoke cleared, the room appeared empty. Suddenly, a man with a white beard and white robe stood before me. I froze. His eyes were fiery. I slowly reached out to touch him, and he disappeared. Then Mom grabbed my hand and all the people in the church came back into focus. I knew the man in the white robe must have been God. This vivid dream has never left me.

Even though I was impressed by that experience, the God that my parents worshipped didn't seem to fit in my world, even when I was a child. Their God was regal and re-mote. He made me feel fearful.

Mom brought such cheer to my heart. I loved watch-ing her cook. Big quarters of onion with the skin on and whole heads of garlic, added to boiling water along with peppercorns, celery ribs and whole carrots were the base for her vegetable stock. "A little of this and a pinch of that" was Mom's way of teaching me her measuring techniques. She had an unfair advantage—her hands were bigger than mine. Wonderful aromas wafted through the house.

I studied her every move. I wanted to learn the way she used different herbs and spices, and her methods of food preparation and baking. I recall sitting on the kitchen counter asking her what she was doing and why she was doing it that way. I even made up excuses to avoid school so I could take cooking lessons from her.

Mom allowed me to experiment sometimes as she laughed at the recipes I concocted. We both laughed hard, especially when some of the food didn't turn out so well. I remember adding lots of cinnamon and lemon juice to one of my earlier pizza sauces. My soups were often too watery, but they had unique flavors—I remember one soup made of cucumbers with ham and honey. But sometimes I enjoyed success. I remember teaching myself to toss pizza dough at the age of seven. My mother didn't welcome the extra flavor added when I dropped the dough on the floor, and I had to practice for a while before I got it right.

My father, however, was unimpressed that his firstborn son spent so much time in the kitchen. "We have three girls in this house who need to know how to cook, not my boys," he would tell Mom. By this time, my three sisters and my brother had come along.

Many years later, I became a cook and then a restaurant owner, creating my own signature recipes and techniques. Those happy days in my mother's kitchen gave me the motivation to explore and enjoy the culinary arts.

My father worked as a butcher. I remember how my brother and I would sit on the front steps of our house every day, anxiously waiting for our father to arrive home from work. Dad would slowly walk down our street, usually carrying a big black garbage bag holding a carcass of meat from his place of work—one of the benefits of his job was that he could take home surplus meat. His pants were always stained with dried blood and his hair always looked messy. When we spotted Dad coming up the street from his long bus ride, my brother and I would race to him. He would laugh and smile watching his two boys. Being taller and bigger, I often won that footrace. Dad would drop his black bag and catch me in his arms. He would kiss my cheek before he would place me over his broad shoulders. He would then bend down, pick up that black bag, and walk towards my little brother. I loved the view from his shoulders. Even more, I loved being his son.

When we were a little older, my father taught us how to sharpen a knife, and explained about different cuts of meats. My brother and I marveled at the way his hands moved when he sharpened the blade of his knife up and down his sharpening steel. "This is how you know it's sharp," Father would say as he trimmed a small patch of hair off his wrist. "Now that's sharp and ready for use!" he'd continue, smiling.

When I was six years old, my naïve bravery got me into trouble. Mother was having tea with Aunt Kanella, who rented the upstairs suite of our home. I wanted to be helpful, so I asked, "Can I go check if the water is boiling for your tea?"

Mom smiled. "Go, but be careful."

I ran into the kitchen and propped a chair against the stove. I stood on the chair, watching the water come to a boil in the cooking pot. Excited to tell Mom that the water was ready, I jumped off the chair, accidently hitting the pot handle on my way down. The scalding water spilled down my legs and onto my feet.

I yelled for my mother to help as I rolled on the floor, trying to escape the pain that flared up as the water spilled down. Within seconds, Mom and Aunty were beside me.

Mom took action. "Kanella, run the cold water in the bathtub. Quickly!"

Our bathroom was next to the kitchen. Aunt Kanella looked frightened. Mom started taking off my clothes and examining my body to see where I was burned. I remember hearing the water rumbling in the tub as the skin from my feet peeled off with my socks. I wasn't sure which was worse, the pain from the scald or the indignation at being naked. My mother told Kanella to call a taxi. The hospital was just a couple of blocks down the street from where we lived. I was in so much pain. Even the cold water splashing on my feet felt hard. Mom kept asking, "How did this happen? God, how did this happen?"

Mom wrapped me in blankets. She whisked me in her arms and ran out into the dark winter's evening. In the cold air, I could see steam rising from my feet. A taxi was waiting for us. Mom told him, "Go, go to the hospital!"

Arriving at the hospital we were met by a team of nurses and doctors. My mother was playing with my hair and kissing my forehead, but they took me from her. "Mama!" I kept yelling as I was being pushed away on a gurney. I saw Mom start to cry. She had done everything she could.

Later that night my father and mother were in my hospital room. "You're going to be okay, my little prince," my father kept saying, repeatedly kissing my hand.

Even so, I was frightened. I felt so alone in the big hospital, where I had to stay for several days. I felt I needed my father to be with me. He lifted my spirits and kept my hopes up. The doctors told me that I required a skin graft on one of my feet and that the other one would be permanently scarred. They said my mother's quick actions—placing my feet in freezing cold water—had prevented my injuries from being worse. Dad visited me every evening after work during the weeks I was in hospital, just to hold my hand and to give me a goodnight kiss. I told Mom that I needed Dad to do that so that I could fall asleep better.

chapter two

My Glimpse
of Greece

When I was eight years old, I believed my father was the strongest, the smartest, the funniest, the most honest, and the handsomest man in the world.

That changed when he turned to alcohol and gambling. My once-hardworking father left his well-paying job at Burns Meats for what he thought would be an easier way of life. He opened a social club for the Greek community. He also loaned lots of money to his Greek buddies to help them to start businesses. Sometimes he just gave them a place to stay, to rest and to eat.

In 1981 our whole family went to Greece for a summer vacation. Dad kept flashing his money around and continued his usual ways of spending it, mostly on booze. This made me mad but I decided to have fun with my brother and cousins instead of allowing Dad's choices to ruin my trip.

My first impression of Mom's village was memorable: all the houses clung precariously to the slanted side of a mountain. We boys felt a little in awe of these people whom we really didn't know. Our mother's father was a tall, stern man. Grandfather watched me like a hawk. Grandmother was a small sweet-looking woman but she had a short temper. While our parents visited with our grandparents, we escaped to explore the village.

It was hard to get to sleep that first night, with strange sounds all around. When we walked out of the house in the morning, the clouds hovered just above our heads.

One afternoon when everyone else was napping, I went to visit a popular site near my grandparents' home: a huge hollow tree. When I peeked inside it, I saw chickens and chicks sitting on straw. I decided I would have some fun. Digging into my pockets I pulled out a pack of matches and lit a couple, tossing them into the straw. Some of the chickens flew away while others seemed content to stay even though flames quickly spread and black smoke filled the hollow of the tree. Before I could enjoy the exciting show, people came running with buckets of water and quickly put out the beautiful fire. A barrage of Greek—lots of swearing and threats—filled my ears. "All the way from Canada he came to burn our tree!" my grandfather roared. I ran to my father for safety while Grandfather's yells filled the air just as the black smoke had filled the tree. The whole town heard about my misdemeanor and I was branded as a villain from Canada. To this very day many remember my little fire incident, but that didn't change my father's status in the village.

Everyone seemed to love my father and he slaughtered many goats and lambs for them. Dad was known to be impassive as he slashed the animals' throats, believing this was the quickest and the most humane way to kill them. "Pick your favorite lamb…" Dad would tell my brother and me in front of Mom's family. But we knew his tricks. Back in Canada, he had often taken us with him to a farm during Easter season. "Which one do you like best?" he would ask. We would foolishly pick out the cutest lambs from the pen and bring them to him. Smiling, he would take them from our hands and, almost before we knew what was happening, he would kill them.

The entire village remembered my mother. People had fond memories of her and often complimented us, saying our looks came from her side of the family. During our time there, my mother took me to a bakery every morning. The bread was so fresh and warm. We always stopped at a deli place to get wonderful cheese called Kasseri.

Every Sunday was a special day for Mom's family. One of her brothers was the priest. Just as I'd imagined, he wore a black robe and had a long beard. My mother greatly admired him and often talked to us about him. He asked me to recite the Lord's Prayer in Greek before bedtime while we stayed at his house. We had learned how to pray and to be proud of our heritage in Greek school back in Canada, but I was far too nervous. I tried to get my brother to say it instead, but I couldn't get out of it and so this became my nightly ritual.

We left my mother's parents' home, and drove nine hours to go visit Dad's side of the family. We wanted to surprise our grandparents who had no idea we were in the country. Our car bounced along the dirt road we took to the field where Grandfather worked. A tall muddy man came walking towards us. "Father!" my dad yelled from the car, and ran to meet him.

My grandfather seemed confused until he recognized my father. "Where is Vasili?" Grandfather asked.

I started towards them and my grandfather met me halfway. He knelt before me and kissed me on the cheek. "You have my name...you have my name," he said, crying, as he hugged me. His house wasn't far from his field so I walked back with him, holding his hand. Grandmother Eleni was so excited to see us.

I didn't know why but we did not stay long with them. I couldn't understand why I didn't get to spend more time with my grandfather, but Dad had rented a house close to a beach only three miles away so that was where we went. I found out later that our father was ashamed to have grown up in a one-room house with six other siblings plus his parents. He did not want us to know that he had grown up in such poverty. My mother had been poor as well, but later in life her parents had become financially stable and better off than my father's parents were.

Both my grandfathers had served and fought in World War II. Grandfather Vasilios was eighteen when he took fifteen-year-old Eleni out of her father's field where she was working, and married her without asking for her father's hand. This was done because Grandma came from a rich family who would never approve of Grandpa. Grandma Eleni's family disowned her, refusing to have anything to do with her until the day she died. Family values and traditions burned brightly on the pages of our history. My brother and I represent the first generation not to serve in the army nor fight in a war in four hundred years. My father thinks every man needs to be disciplined by the army and taught to defend his country, but I don't think he's disappointed I never enlisted.

Before we returned to Canada, we visited our father's favorite cousin, a bishop in Athens. This cousin, together with seven other priests, had performed my parents' marriage ceremony. Dad often spoke to us about how much he respected and loved this cousin. Bishop Athanasios (Ilias) Vasilopoulos was a tall man with a salt-and-pepper beard. As I stared up at him, he placed one big hand on my brother's head and one on mine. He began to pray over us. I felt electricity racing through my body. The entire experience was eerie. Even though my brother did not seem fazed, I have never forgotten it.

I loved our time in Greece but even in our trip we saw some small clues to what would become my father's struggles. Only later would those struggles become known. Could we have recognized the clues? Could we have avoided some of the pain? Those burning questions are still unanswered.

chapter three

Pain from the Past

A young boy waited nervously near a shop in the little Greek village. It was the evening of August 20, 1961. A rusty old van finally appeared. The lad who would one day become my father had been dreaming about the moment when that van would arrive. The van was driven by his uncle, Tom, a clothing merchant who sold his wares to most of the towns in the area. When my father's uncle stopped to go into a store nearby, the young boy jumped into the van and hid under the clothes and boxes, his heart pounding. He thought to himself, *In six hours I will be in Athens!*

Here's how he remembered it: *My father was often angry with me for reasons I was never told. Two years earlier I had forgotten to tie up our goat in the shade before noon came. The scorching heat and the lack of water led to the goat's death. It had been the only source of milk for our family. I didn't think of that. It was such a beautiful hot day and I was caught up in child's play. Only twelve years old, I was fast, but not as fast as Father. He chased me for what seemed like miles, but eventually he caught me when*

I tripped and hit the ground. He gave my little head a swift kick with his large boot. Then he placed his foot on my neck, pinning me to the ground. As I gasped for breath, my mind raced in search of a reason for this outpouring of his rage. I thought I would die and half-wished I could. Somehow, I lived.

When I reached my fourteenth birthday I had had enough. That is why I hid in my uncle's van. I wanted freedom from fear of my father and no cost would be too great to get it. Looking back at my younger years, I wonder how I ever made it. I wish I could have asked him, "Why, Daddy?"

My mother's upbringing was not perfect either. When she was eight years old, her father gave her up for adoption to a wealthy family who could not have children of their own. This was supposed to allow her to break away from poverty. At least that is what she was told. Upset and terrified, my mother had no choice in her parents' decision.

The woman who became her new mother put her to work immediately. My mother felt like a slave in this big new home in Athens. Yes, her new mother bought her fancy dresses and toys, but that could not make up for the sting of anger directed at her. Slaps, pinches and ridicule were that woman's way of teaching my mother right from wrong. The doctor who became Mom's new father never paid attention to her.

"Why did my daddy give me to these people?" the girl who would become my mother asked herself. Every night she would stare out of her bedroom window, crying and hoping that her father would come rescue her. The beatings from this new mother intensified as time went on. No one was there to help until one day her sister Maria came to visit her in Athens. "Andigoni, is everything okay?" Maria asked, startled by the bruises and marks she saw on her sister's little body. My mother lied and nodded her head, fearing her new mother was listening in on their conversation.

When the fall season came, she made her escape. One night while everyone was asleep, she snuck out of the house and jumped on a bus. Apparently, the bus driver realized she needed help, for he let her get on the bus and even helped her find the neighborhood where some family members lived. Scared and alone, she made her way to a relative's place. It sounds crazy now that she could manage to get there, but it makes me realize how frightened that little eight-year-old must have been. No wonder my mother still has so much inner strength!

Both of my parents returned home to live with their parents for a few years. But, before long, they each returned to the big city of Athens. In 1966, they met at a butcher shop where my father worked. They courted for a year until the army drafted my father for two years of service. That same year the king of Greece was overthrown and was replaced by a dictator. Some Greeks fled to Canada while others went to America. As soon as Dad finished his army term, my parents got married, in the summer of 1969. In November of that year, my mother pregnant with me, they fled to Winnipeg, Manitoba. My mother's sister Maria and her husband, Christo, already lived in Canada. Thanks to them, Dad had a job waiting for him at a meat plant. He was assured that the work would pay well.

If only our family's return to Canada after the holiday in Greece had led to such positive results as our parents' initial arrival.

chapter four

Problems and Possibilities

Things began to change when we got back to Winnipeg. Some of the scary things that happened were the results of our own childish pranks.

Shortly after our arrival back from Greece our mother took all five of us children shopping for school clothes and supplies. As usual, we walked to the store together, holding hands. Many years later I learned Mom deliberately chose to walk so we would be tuckered out when we got home. As children we loved horsing around, playing tag or hide-and-seek in those big department stores. Sometimes I took the clothes off the mannequins and put them on myself, pretending I was one of them. I often scared customers who walked by with a loud sneeze or a cough. I was usually rewarded with a scream or yelp, and I laughed hysterically at the reactions I got. Most often these customers saw the humor in the situation and laughed with me. Now, I confess I was being a brat.

The memory of that shopping trip with my mother still affects me. We were in one of the city's downtown department stores when I heard an ear-piercing scream. Two of my sisters had been fooling around near the escalator, some distance from where the rest of us were playing. Later, they remembered that a customer had cautioned them to watch their fingers as she walked onto the escalator.

One of my sisters didn't take the lady's remark seriously. Instead, she tried to see how far down her hand could go without being caught in the moving plastic rail. Within seconds it happened: her hand was caught. Her screams caused panic on the entire second floor, and still echo in my ears whenever I walk through department stores.

People came running from every direction. I broke through the crowd that was standing by helplessly, watching my sister stuck in the escalator and in pain. Acting on impulse, I grasped her forearm with both hands and, somehow, I yanked her hand loose. We both rolled backwards. As we scrambled to our feet, the crowd cheered to see that her hand was hardly injured. A small patch of skin from the side of one of her fingers had been rubbed off but that was all. Mom arrived, breaking through the bystanders to see my sister and I huddled on the floor, hugging each other. My mother grabbed my sister, kissing her and staring at me.

The department manager quickly ushered our family to his office. Closing the door behind us, he begged my mother not to take legal action. Not knowing her rights in this country, Mom complied. Not long afterwards, warning stickers appeared all over that department store's escalators. That made us realize the incident had been far more serious than we could have imagined.

It's normal for kids to get hurt when they do silly things, but there were other dangers, too. Our once-safe West End Winnipeg neighborhood had deteriorated during my teen years. There were signs of a downward spiral inside our house, too.

Dad discovered that the people he had left in charge of his business had no integrity. Customers reported seeing staff pocketing money from the till after their shifts ended, but Dad refused to believe that anyone would try to scam him, and kept those people on staff until he lost all his money and his business had fallen apart. He had loaned out lots of money to friends who were unwilling to pay back a dime. When it became clear that his buddies never really were his friends, he was deeply hurt. He became bitter and depressed, and taught us never to trust anyone and especially never to lend money to friends.

The Dad I had known was fading away: his smiles and his laughter were gone, his commitment to honesty weakened, and he seemed to lose all interest in my siblings and me. Our home life deteriorated quickly. I no longer felt confident that my father would protect me.

A few significant things happened to me when I turned fourteen. The first was that I discovered a passion for football. I spent hours after school in the field, throwing the ball in different directions and at different speeds. I practiced in the rain, on windy days, and even in the dead of winter. Like many young men, I suppose, I was determined to be an NFL quarterback. I dreamed of playing for the Dallas Cowboys. Dad didn't seem to be impressed. He never really told me what he thought I should consider becoming when I got older. All he said was, "Make sure it pays well!"

The second thing that happened that year was that my English teacher took great interest in me. She encouraged me to write. She found my short stories humorous and told me that one day, people would love to read my stories. It seemed odd to me that she liked them since I poked fun at her and other teachers in those stories. She posted our stories on the back wall for other students to read. My stories were popular, especially among the nerdy students. I guess they were amused that I had nerve to make fun of our teachers.

Not all my teachers were as encouraging as she was. One teacher got very upset with me, and I think it was because I had taken an interest in one of the eighth-grade girls. All of us kids knew that this male teacher had a crush on the girl, and we thought that was sick. One day during recess, that girl and I were chasing each other in the hallway and ended up in the classroom. My teacher grabbed me by my neck, holding me so tightly that his dirty nails dug into my skin. He put me up against the wall in front of my entire class and watched me fight to breathe. I slapped his hand over and over, trying to escape his grip. I felt my face get hot as my embarrassment rose. I couldn't do anything, except hope the humiliation would end quickly. He seemed to take pleasure in watching me squirm and suffer. No one came to help me.

When he finally released his grip, I bolted out of the classroom and right out of the school.

When I walked into the house, Dad confronted me. "What's that on your neck?" he asked, turning my head from side to side. His face contorted as concern changed to rage. He demanded to know how I had gotten the marks.

"My teacher did it!"

My father grabbed my hand and dragged me back to school. He didn't say a word to me all the way there. I was afraid that he would blame me, but he didn't. We barged into the principal's office where my father demanded an explanation for the teacher harming a teenaged boy. Witnesses had reported the incident to the principal, and he had already sent the teacher home.

My father defended me! The one who had once loved me, the one I used to look up to was not blaming me for anything. Sadly, though, I was still unwilling to forgive him for all the hurt that he himself had brought into our family.

I felt vindicated when the teacher was transferred to a different school and then was permanently released from being a teacher the following year. However, anger was simmering inside me.

chapter five

Search for Significance

Going to the beach was our family's only getaway, although those excursions hardly ever included my father. One beach day turned out to be a nightmare. We had gone to Birds Hill, a popular beach. My cousin George and my brother, George, went off swimming across the man-made lake without adult supervision. Neither of them was strong enough to make it to the other side. Another cousin, Demetre, George's older brother, and a teenage girl spotted them struggling. Demetre and the girl swam frantically toward the floundering boys. I followed, but I did not have the speed to make it to the scene in time. By the time I arrived, my cousin and brother had been rescued. This experience showed me that I wasn't strong enough or fast enough to be of help to someone in need.

Then, during my last year in junior high school, another near-drowning occurred during a class camping trip. We were being taught how to canoe. Before we knew what happened, Jenny, our class clown, went overboard. She began screaming and thrashing around in the water. The teachers told us to stay in our canoes but I couldn't bear to watch this poor girl floundering helplessly. Jenny's life jacket popped loose and she started going under. I threw off my life jacket and jumped into the cold water. I swam to the spot where I had last seen her. Taking a deep breath, I went under the water and managed to find her. I tried to hold her head above the water as I dog-paddled. In her panic to stay afloat, she pushed me under the water. By the time the other canoes arrived to save us, my lungs were burning and I kept coughing up water. Students were crying and some of the teachers were obviously upset with me for not following orders, but I didn't care.

To Dad's delight, I began to bring girls home—it seemed important to Dad that his sons became womanizers. He encouraged us boys to engage in promiscuous behavior under his roof, even though this disgusted my mom and my sisters. My parents often argued and my mom ended up in tears.

Before long, I was leading my brother down the same dark path my father was taking. My sisters and I never really got along; I simply didn't care enough about them at that time and didn't make any effort to get to know them.

When I entered high school, I was finally old enough to try out for the football team, something I hoped would win my father's approval. But he didn't come to a single practice. One day, I walked off the field for the last time. I simply gave up and never pursued my dream. I tried so hard to make my father proud of me, but he just didn't seem to care.

I started skipping school, stealing clothes, drinking, smoking, and using drugs and eventually dropped out of school.

When I turned eighteen, my father quit drinking. While that seemed like a good thing, there were other problems. Dad was easily agitated and talked about strange things he could see. Maybe that's what led him to quit. Even when he was sober, my father often talked down to me and made me feel worthless. He made it clear that I was a *big* disappointment to him.

One day when I came home he started yelling at me again, but this time I decided I wasn't going to take it. I didn't want his abuse anymore. We got into a swearing and shoving match and things got out of control. He started smashing furniture. He grabbed a garden shovel from behind the front door and swung it at me. He wasn't just threatening to scare me—I was sure he wanted to kill me. With one of his swings, I felt the wind of the shovel's blade on my neck. That was enough for me. I bombarded him with punches, striking him even as he begged me to stop. He tried to get away, stumbling to the bedroom. This was the first time I had seen my father afraid of me.

When I had finished punishing him for all the cruel things he had done to my family, and to me, I stopped. He was curled up on his bed, crying. I stood there, looking down at him, my fists still clenched and my breathing heavy after the exertion. I turned to leave the house. I despised myself for hitting my own father.

I went to stay with my Aunt Maria and Uncle Christo. They pleaded with me to tell them what had happened between my father and me. The next day I phoned my mother.

She wept as we spoke. "How could you do such a thing to your own father?"

"He tried to kill me." I was crying too.

"Your father is in the hospital and he's asking to see you."

"Why?"

"Please come home and we will both go see him together."

"I don't want to ever see him!"

"Please… please come with me."

I couldn't bear to hear Mom cry so I agreed to come. When I arrived at the hospital, I found out my father was in the psychiatric ward. "What are we doing here?" I asked my mom, "Why is he at this hospital?"

She kept silent. We went through security doors and then I saw my dad playing a game of pool with other patients and my siblings. He spotted me and walked towards me with open arms as tears ran down his face. He was horribly bruised. I froze as he put his arms around me and gave me a kiss on the cheek.

I couldn't put my arms around him. I couldn't move. I turned and walked away from him.

"Vasili! Come back here," he cried.

I ran home. Seeing the room where we fought still in shambles, I bolted up the stairs and headed for the bathroom. I found a package of new disposable plastic razors, broke off the protective plastic, and started slashing my wrists. I felt a burning sensation with every slash. Bright red blood flowed down my wrists. I walked into my bedroom and stared out my window, looking at the traffic going by below. I felt like a monster. Repeatedly I asked the agonizing question, "Who could do what I did to my father?"

I looked down and noticed blood between my fingers and on the floor. Suddenly I broke out of the spell of suicide. I realized I wanted to live. *My mother would die if I died now.* I grabbed towels to stanch the flow of blood, then called a friend and told him what I had done. When he arrived to take me to the hospital, I had already cleaned up the mess I had made.

At the hospital, I was admitted promptly after I told them what I had done to myself. The nurse asked to see my wrists. There were only faint scratches there. I shook my head in disbelief. "I don't know why there is nothing there," I told the nurse. I felt really dumb! They brought a psychiatrist and his students to assess me. I refused to answer many of their questions, afraid of becoming their guinea pig. When they left me alone, I got up and snuck out of the hospital.

chapter six

Desperate Measures

My family wasn't the same anymore. I decided I would no longer call my father "Dad" but would use his first name, Andy. I refused to listen to him, and did as I pleased. I set a terrible example to my siblings, but I didn't care. "Andy" and I continued our yelling matches after he got out of the hospital. He took every opportunity to throw in my face the fact I had beaten him up.

"You should have had my father!" Andy would yell. "My father would have given you a beating that you would never forget!"

"No, he wouldn't, because he would know he'd get back double of what you got!" was my standard reply.

We were told that my father had a mental illness called bipolar disorder, but I was merciless toward him, thinking he would use his diagnosis as an excuse to be even more pitiful, another reason to ignore his family.

I was no more responsible than he was: during my last teenaged year, in 1989, I got a girlfriend pregnant. I tried to do what I thought was the right thing by moving in together in a nice apartment. My mother was not pleased. She insisted I get married and start being a man. I ignored her.

The following year, my father opened another Greek social club that catered to gambling and drinking. I went to work for him, and quickly took interest in his drug-dealing patrons. Even if I didn't respect him, I was adopting my father's liking for money. I envied those drug dealers for all the money and women they had. I wanted what they had—expensive gold jewelry and fancy cars. I was having a hard time making ends meet, so one of my father's friends took me under his wing, teaching me how to navigate the lucrative drug world. In a very short time, I had become a drug dealer, something my father despised.

My daughter was born in the summer of 1990. She was such a great joy to me. My thoughts were often consumed with her well-being. I wanted to get out of the drug world, but it was too hard to give up the easy money. One night I received a call from a drug addict at a party. The three-a.m. call alarmed my girlfriend. She had no idea what I was doing on the side to make money. I didn't have a good feeling about that call, but I needed the money. The addict gave me a code for the size of his drug order. The amount sounded excessive for this guy. He never had that kind of money so I brought him only half the drugs he wanted. Against my better instincts, I went to the party. Things quickly went wrong. My customer's bug-eyed look told me that he'd been smoking crack cocaine. He pulled out a gun with trembling hands and pointed it at my head.

"Give me all your drugs!" he rasped.

"Be cool... It's in my pocket," I replied, thinking about my little girl growing up without a father. He searched my pockets and patted me down.

"Where's the rest?" His face was only inches from mine. I was caught and I knew it.

"I don't have any more with me." I had to think fast. "I can get you some more, but that means you'll have to let me live."

His gun shook in front of my face as he tried staring me down.

Why did I come here tonight?

"I could kill you right now!" he blasted.

Enraged at his antics, I wanted to kill this punk for threatening me in front of his friends, but I had to stay cool. "Do you want more drugs or not!" I asked.

He slowly put his gun down, laughing crazily. "I like you, man. You're all right... you're all right."

I slowly walked out of the house expecting to be shot in the back. Nothing happened and I never went to that house again.

I thought about getting my revenge, but I didn't get a chance to follow through on my plans because shortly after that night, the RCMP busted me. I had carelessly sold drugs to an informant a few months previously. The informant had come to my father's social club and approached me at the bar where I was working. He introduced himself as a car salesman. He said I would look good driving a Corvette he had on his car lot. Then he asked if a certain drug dealer had stopped by yet. I foolishly tried to "cut" that drug dealer's grass by trying to get this car salesman to be my new customer instead. I was twenty years old. The trap was set and I was naïve enough to step right into it.

I had already introduced my little brother to the world of drugs and womanizing. My brother had always looked up to me. I tried to justify myself, claiming I was trying to get us out of poverty and despair, but I was just looking for an easy excuse and was simply following the example my father had set. When I got busted, I disgraced my family. The incident was written up in the newspapers and televised on the evening news. All this exposure caused my mother a lot of distress. Of the dozens of people busted by this informant, I was the youngest. Everyone else was over thirty-five. The RCMP took a great interest in me because I was involved at such a young age with this filthy drug organization they labeled The Brazil Mar Organization.

I had also spent some of my teen years working in the hospitality industry. One of the places I worked at was a Greek family's restaurant. I was their delivery driver and pizza-maker. When they found out I had been charged with criminal offences, they fired me. I thought my boss was a self-righteous coward for releasing me from my job simply because I had been charged with a crime.

My relationship with my girlfriend fell apart and I slowly lost visitation rights to my daughter.

I tried to get my drug charges dropped, and the delay lasted five years, but on my twenty-fifth birthday in 1995, I was sentenced to a federal penitentiary for two years and a day. I was furious at my lawyer's ineffective work on my behalf. My family and friends who were present for the sentencing started sobbing. The guards quickly placed handcuffs on my wrists and shackles on my ankles. Mom ran to me and wrapped her arms around my neck as her cries turned to wails of grief. My siblings reached out, wanting to hug and kiss me but the guards asked them to back away. I just wanted to get out of that courtroom. "Andy" stared at me with tears running down his face. He opened his arms to hug me.

I looked at him and said, "Get out of my way and don't touch me!"

"Why?" my father pleaded.

"Because you know how I feel about you. Now move!"

He hung his head and moved aside as I walked past him with the prison guards.

During those years of waiting for the courts, I had desperately tried searching for God. I wrote poems and read the Bible my cousin George gave me but somehow, I could not connect with Him. The night before my sentencing, I had called my cousin George whose family were caretakers of the Greek Orthodox Church. They let me into the darkened building. I approached the altar, staring up at Jesus and all the pictures of the saints. I fell to my knees and wept, confessing all my wrongs and begging God not to let me go to jail. I was desperate.

I also asked God to help me have the relationship with my daughter I desperately wanted. I had fought hard to get visitation rights with my daughter but I was only allowed supervised visits. It seemed like God had no more interest in me than my father.

In prison, I thought back to the last time I had seen my little girl. After my supervised visit, I had made her a tiny snowman and put it on a cast-iron stair. She had stared at it and smiled as I waved goodbye. I knew I would never forget that but I wondered if I would ever see her again.

chapter seven

Doing Time

While in prison I kept trying to find God, but I couldn't. It was easier for me to blame Him for all my troubles.

My grandfather, Vasilios, back in Greece, was very sick. I dreamed of going back there to see him when I got out of jail, but he died a month after I was imprisoned. Dad and Grandfather didn't get a chance to make things right between them. This hurt me very much and made me angry. I think I was angry because I feared my relationship with my father would probably end up the same way.

I spent two weeks in the remand center before I was transferred to Stony Mountain Federal Penitentiary. Before leaving the remand center, two guards strip-searched me. I noticed that the two inmates I would be travelling with did not have to undergo this humiliating process and this made me mad. (In prison, I was often strip-searched, especially after visits from family and friends.)

I'll never forget that van ride to Stony Mountain. The prisoners sat in the back, shackled and handcuffed, while the guards rode safely in the front. I tried to ignore the scary-looking inmates but they kept laughing and bragging about their gruesome crime. The terrible thing was that they had murdered one of the customers who used to come into my father's social club. I kept my head bowed, afraid of making eye contact with them. After what seemed like hours of travelling toward Stony Mountain, one of the inmates spotted the prison and said, "Home sweet home!" and they both laughed again.

I looked out of the back window of the van and finally saw the place where I would serve my sentence. I had never seen it before. It looked haunted and very cold. As soon as I arrived at Stony Mountain, I had to endure another strip-search. Then someone took my mug shot, and I was fingerprinted and given an inmate number. Each step in the process seemed to mock me. Now I had a criminal record, and this label would brand me across the country. I would not be able to get away from it no matter where in Canada I went.

Prison quickly changes a man. You see and hear so much evil. It is disgusting, and hits you especially hard the first night before bed. Grown men's screams and the cries of madmen echo through the cellblocks. Other inmates swear at the noisy ones to shut up, only adding to the din. Most of the men in prison are ruthless. Later I learned that many of them had grown up without fathers, and I wonder if that didn't have a big influence on the way they turned out. They quarrel over the stupidest things and create even stupider rules in prison. I had to fight to have a seat to sit down to have a meal, because apparently even the chairs are claimed.

Mealtime in prison is very tense. It is just one more frightening experience. It is not a time to relax. You have no time to enjoy your meal. By the way, they don't serve steaks or fine meals. They do load up your diet with lots of junk food and sweets that give off the appearance that you eat well in prison but compared to what I was accustomed to at home, it was very much inferior.

Some men stare at you; their devilish eyes suggest they are contemplating how to harm you while they watch you eat. Contrary to foolish stereotypes, the most dangerous place in prison is your cell. I was advised by a cellmate to remove one of my pant legs if I had to sit to go to the bathroom. Otherwise, I would be hobbled and wouldn't be able to stand to defend myself if I was attacked.

All prisoners learn to look down when they walk by another cell that has bedcovers over the bars or doors. It usually means someone is being violently attacked or taken advantage of.

The only stereotype I found to be true was the statement: "You never forget the sound of slamming doors"— those infamous electrical doors that slam behind you as you enter different chambers of the prison. Even as I write this, it seems I faintly hear one closing behind me.

Fortunately, since I was serving time for a drug beef (drug trafficking), the other inmates left me alone. But the guards didn't. The guards consistently strip-searched me for drugs after visits. That made it more sickening to watch other inmates, who packed drugs in their own bodies, waddling past me as they headed for their cells, because I knew they were getting away with their smuggling.

I begged my family not to visit me. I could see the fear and worry in their eyes, telling me they realized I was spending time in a very dangerous place. Often, we all stared at each other, not knowing what to say. Mom missed only one visit despite my many pleas for her to stay home.

Prisoners who are young are more vulnerable to being used as a "girlfriend." I felt sorry for these vulnerable, scared young men. They were easy to spot because of their style of dress—wearing their gangster pants halfway down, exposing their boxer shorts. These young guys had their gang symbols tattooed on their arms and bodies, making them easy targets for the inmates to get their revenge on them. Lockdowns and strip-searches are common things in prison, and so is selling drugs and having conjugal visits with girlfriends or spouses.

Every so often a cellblock was shut down. That meant all inmates were ordered back to their cells in a certain unit of the prison. A group of guards would come into our cellblock with dogs, wearing gloves. The guards would call us out of our cells one by one, and strip-search us in front of everyone. Then they would enter our cells with the dogs, searching for drugs or weapons.

One day they found more than thirty shanks in our cellblock. Shanks are weapons formed from unusual objects like toothbrushes or aluminum pop cans. The criminal mind can conjure up ways of making weapons out of items you would never think of as potential arms. I knew that prison was not a safe place, and that day confirmed it for me, although I realized that most of these shanks were made for inmates to defend themselves, not necessarily to harm others.

Another disturbing thing many people are not aware of, and which inmates don't talk about, is that guards pass condoms to the inmates. The first time this happened to me, I smirked at the guard, "For what?"

"You never know," he replied, laughing, as he walked away.

I didn't get his warped humor until later that day. The condoms are for inmates to use in order to engage in safe sex with one another.

Some guards appeared not to care about the safety of the inmates. Who can blame them? I found out that rapists and pedophiles have protection rights in prison and are separated from the main population of the inmates for fear that they will be harmed or killed. These types of disturbed inmates were the only ones to have their own cells, unlike the other inmates like me who each had a cellmate.

In prison, I often thought about my daughter. She gave me a reason to live and something to hope for but God didn't seem very concerned about my desire to see my little girl. I saw my daughter only once while I was in jail. This was when her mother told me she was moving to a different province.

The good thing about prison was that it helped me see who my true friends were. Sadly, I found out that most of them were users. Like my father, I found out the hard way what kind of people these friends were.

Overall, my stay in prison gave me a glimpse of what some people would call hell. It didn't do anything to deter my thinking about being a drug dealer; it just made me hate life more than before.

When I got out, I fought hard to see my little girl who was five years old by then, but it wasn't easy. Because I have a criminal record and because her mother and I lived in different provinces, it was impossible to make any headway in the court system. I defaulted to my crazy, drug-dealing life.

chapter eight

Followed and Condemned by My Past Life

When I got out of prison, I went to the Greek Orthodox Church with my cousin George. He wanted me to attend a Bible study with him. I enjoyed it but as I was leaving, I overheard two Greek men in the gated, outer courtyard of the church talking about me. One of them said, "When someone loses his reputation in this church, it's very hard to get it back." I glared at them and they looked the other way. That was it. No more God stuff for me. I was going to figure out life on my own. I partied harder than ever, beat up men in bars and at parties, womanized and sold drugs more relentlessly than ever. For six years I lived life on the edge.

My mother never stopped praying for me, as she feared the worst for me. Although I could never fool her, it wasn't in her nature to confront me. I think she was a little afraid of me, too. My father had given up all hope in me. We hardly spoke unless it was to tell each other off.

In 1997, my parents opened a restaurant in MacGregor, a town in western Manitoba. My brother and I went to work with them. In the beginning the restaurant did very well. Then we posted a review on our front door from a previous restaurant my parents had owned. The food critic had praised my mother's cooking, giving her four stars out of a possible five, and had commented on the friendly service at George's Ouzeri. Our names were posted on this review and that's when things went downhill. My past caught up to my family as the locals found out about my criminal record. Our customers, many of whom were Christians, decided to shun our restaurant. This hurt us deeply and deepened my distrust for God and the church. It seemed that the Greeks who had said it was hard to get a reputation back were right.

When my parents lost the restaurant in MacGregor, I tried to open my own restaurant in another town. My new business did not succeed. My landlord and I had agreed in writing that I was supposed to have living accommodations above the restaurant, but the day I was to take possession of the apartment, he gave me a sob story, saying he did not have the heart to boot out the family that was living there. Three months earlier he had told me that he was looking forward to kicking them out because the teenagers had gone wild and it was time for them to go. This reversal left me commuting seven days a week. After a few months, I was tired and had spent too much money on gas between the city and restaurant, so I arranged for a meeting to discuss compensation with my landlord. It ended with him demanding that I give him the keys to my restaurant if I wasn't happy. I refused and the following day I was locked out. I decided to sue him but it took years to set up a court date.

That wasn't my only problem. When I got locked out of my restaurant I went to work in the same meat plant my father had worked in when he first came to Canada. My father had worked on the "Kill Floor," a department many other workers refused to work in. I worked in "Cutting" and in "Packaging."

The place was cold and it stank. As I walked through the cold plant, I envisioned my father working all those long hours. My heart wept thinking about him and the ridicule he had faced. I thought about how he had just kept pressing on, doing whatever it took to support his family. I never told him then that I appreciated what he did for me and for the rest of our family.

Working at the meat plant brought back so many good childhood memories of Dad that I had forgotten, but Memory Lane ended when I had a freak accident: it is hard to imagine but one day half a hog carcass shot off the ramp and drilled me on my lower back as I stood, facing away from the ramp. I was on Workers Compensation for almost three months until their doctor ruled that I had recovered and was again ready for work.

During the injury period, I drank a lot and did drugs frequently to try to numb the extreme pain. Eventually a friend recommended that I try steroids. Within two weeks the pain started to subside. It was great to have relief but the side effects—episodes of rage—made me realize the relief was costly. After abusing my body with steroids for a few months, I weaned myself from them and never tried steroids again. (I had another back injury in 2010 at a different place of work, but this time steroids aren't an option for coping with the intense chronic pain. Now I wait for God's healing and the help of doctors to correct this injury.)

By 2000, my drug habits had taken over my life. I had become a hard-core drug addict. I had my own pad in the West End, and no one could tell me what to do. I started doing cocaine on my own for days on end. I had broken the drug dealers' code of ethics: never become your own best customer. I knew I was on a dangerous road, but I just didn't care anymore. Nothing was exciting—even women. Drinking made me depressed, and smoking burned my lungs. My word carried no weight anymore on the streets because I often lied to get my drug fixes. Beating people up and partying had become dull. Nothing I did brought me pleasure, so I wanted to end it all. I snorted lots of cocaine for nights on end, sleeping only briefly during the day. I was afraid to go to sleep sober at night, afraid of what I had become. I couldn't look at myself in the mirror without wanting to cry or smash it.

"Who am I?" I finally asked myself one evening before starting what I believed would be my last drug binge. I had decided to take drugs until my heart could not take it anymore. As usual I had crazy rave music playing on my CD player. I opened my bag of cocaine and spilled it on my coffee table. I crushed the big rocks into a fine powder with a plastic bankcard. I rolled up a twenty-dollar bill. I made thick lines of cocaine. I was not going to do little teasing lines that would give me only short buzzes. *I might as well go out with a bang.* With each snort, I felt my nose burning, and my thoughts ran wild.

Suddenly I panicked. Hours had gone by and I didn't know what time it was. Shadowy figures filled the room. In the background, I heard a song called "Dance with the Devil." My heart was racing and the hairs on my body rose. I knew there was a dark presence in my home. I had felt a similar presence many years before, as a boy in my parents' home. It was even scarier now. Paranoia set in. I scrambled to get out of that place. It felt like the forces of hell had invaded the room and I was terrified.

chapter nine

Unseen Terror

When I opened the back door to get out, I was nearly blinded by the bright daylight. I had no idea how many hours had passed or even what day it was. The constant noise of street life greeted me, and the freezing wind caught me off guard. In my unsteadiness, I landed on the frozen ground. It was an insanely cold January day in Winnipeg. I fought to get my footing on a patch of ice, but my drug-ravaged, weakened body just wouldn't let me stand up. The clamor of traffic blared about my ears. When I finally got my footing, I looked at the palms of my hands. I had cut them when I fell and they stung despite the cold.

My heart was racing faster and faster. I was afraid that I didn't have much time before it exploded. I knew I didn't want to die in my own home. For some reason, I wanted to die in my old bedroom at my parents' home, about ten blocks away.

As I stumbled toward my parents' house, old memories began to surface. Looking back now, I wonder if God was using my helpless state to cleanse my soul of pain from my past.

I found myself on the path that I used to take home from elementary school. Terrible memories of childhood beatings arose to the surface.

I recalled an incident at the corner store. My little brother and I had been terrified to walk home from Wellington Elementary School because we were constantly bullied by a boy named Mikey and his cronies. One summer's day just before I entered junior high school, something happened to change that. My brother and I were at the corner grocery store on our street. Before we could buy the candy we had come for, Mikey entered the store, and began to taunt my brother. Without hesitation, I attacked, hitting him square in the face. As Mikey fell backwards, he knocked down the chip stand behind him. The grocery clerk yelled at us to stop and told us to get out. I don't know if it was the rage on my face or the shock of being knocked down, but Mikey looked terrified. My brother's expression showed a mix of surprise and something like pleasure. From that day forward I feared no one—except my father.

As I kept walking, another childhood memory involving my brother came into focus. I had been playing hopscotch on the school grounds with one of my cousins when I heard a thump. A car sped away, revealing my baby brother lying on the ground. I ran to him and then knelt, looking at his motionless body. I looked up at my front yard and was horrified to see that I had left the gate open. I raced to the back yard where my mom was hanging clothes to dry. I cried out, "The baby has been hit by a car!" In a split second, Mom turned and bolted to the scene. She cradled my brother in her arms as though he was a little rag doll.

"Christe mou!" ("My Christ!") my mother cried. Her outburst startled the neighbors who had hurried out of their homes when they heard the commotion. They stood around awkwardly, not knowing what to do. Off in the distance I could see my mother's sister Maria and her son Demetre heading our way. My aunt heard my mother's chilling cries and ran to her. She grabbed my little brother's lifeless body and shook him. Her repeated cries of "Christe mou!" joined with Mom's sobs.

Then an amazing thing happened. Blood spurted out of one of my brother's ears and he whimpered. My mom looked up at the sound, and snatched my brother out of her sister's arms. She kept kissing him as he cried louder. The ambulance arrived to take my mother and brother to the hospital. I was left behind with my aunt and cousins.

As I approached my parents' street, that memory faded away, only to be replaced by another one. This memory involved my baby sister. She was just eighteen months old at the time, around the same age as my brother had been when he nearly died. The kids on my block were playing hide-and-seek. I hid high up in the elm trees fronting our street, observing the kids from above, seeing them getting tagged out one by one. I wanted to be the hero saving the bunch. Suddenly a much bigger challenge was before me. As I came down the tree, I spotted my baby sister, wearing just her diaper, heading into traffic. I practically jumped down the tree, and ran right past the kids with whom I had been playing. I needed to save her! My sister entered the curb lane as a car was heading straight for her. I darted from between the parked cars, snatching my sister up in my arms, and then turned, expecting to be hit. All I heard was screeching brakes. I braced for impact, still holding my sister tightly in my arms. Death missed its opportunity again. I had blamed myself for forgetting to shut the gate for my brother. This time I was determined that I would prevent anything happening to my little sister.

I heard a car door opening and then slamming shut. "What were you thinking?" a lady yelled at me. When I turned to face her, she saw my baby sister. Trembling, the lady quickly placed her fingers over her mouth. "Oh my God… are you all right?" she cried.

My drug haze of a journey to my parents' home was now nearly over. I spotted my father at the open door.

Father looked closely at me. "Vasili," he called out.

He was the last person I wanted to see so I kept walking in the freezing cold. The wind carried his angry words to me. "Are you on drugs?"

I was losing strength. The sound of snow crunching under the soles of my feet kept me going but my heart was beating faster than ever. Time was now against me. I turned down the end of the street and stumbled along the back lane, heading back to my parents' house. *If my father is still there, I'll shove him out of my way and run up the stairs to my old bedroom,* I thought.

Somehow, I made it back to the house. My toes were numb and my ears were burning. My tongue was dry and my eyes felt like they were going to bulge out of my head. The back door was shut in a futile attempt to keep out the cold, so I had to go around to the front again. I walked up the front steps, fumbling to find the key in my pocket. I found it, turned the lock and crept upstairs as quietly as I could. I didn't dare stop until I had made it into my old bedroom. I locked that door behind me, gasping for breath.

The shadowy figures I had seen before reappeared. The room had an unnatural chill. I was not alone. I feared that God would punish me for all my wrongs, so I quickly took off my jacket and knelt beside my bed. I prayed, "God, would you forgive me for the terrible life that I have led?" Then I rolled onto my bed and closed my eyes. Everything became dark. I felt like I was drowning. My lungs were burning and my eyes felt tired and heavy. I could hear my heart beat— it was no longer fast. The beat became faint and all the madness and pain stopped. I didn't want to fight for my life. I preferred staying in this state of weightlessness. There was not much to fight for, I thought.

I was amazed to wake up the next morning.

chapter ten

Dissatisfaction

From that day on, I would never do drugs by myself. I wanted the company of friends or partygoers, and for them to participate with me, but it was never the same. Inevitably I would feel guilty and I got bored very easily. My urge for drugs and partying hard was fading. I couldn't quite figure out what was happening inside me, but it seemed as if something bigger or someone stronger than me was challenging my addiction. I felt something unfamiliar inside, a sense of dissatisfaction with drugs.

In the summer of 2001, I got involved with a woman who was studying to be a lawyer and who hated drugs. Her influence seemed to help me to change for the better. Believing she was the one for me, I moved in with her.

One day while she was in class, I started fiddling with her computer. I didn't really know how to type and I'm not sure where the idea came from but I felt like writing a fantasy book. It was hard—I had forgotten how to write creatively—but my girlfriend encouraged me to continue writing even though I was just recording loads of thoughts that flitted through my mind. The story was set in a medieval time, with characters that face the issues men face today. In three weeks, I wrote two hundred pages. I couldn't shut my mind off. There was so much I needed to let out. The story took on a life of its own, but when God became connected with the main character, I started to worry.

I thought of calling my cousin George although we hadn't talked in years. All I knew was he had been educated, had married and had become a priest. When he heard my voice on the phone, he sounded happy. He quickly agreed to come visit. We talked for a couple of hours. I found out I had been wrong about one thing: he was not a priest but an assistant pastor. When I heard that, I guessed his church didn't have pictures of saints and big chandeliers or giant candles. Unlike the priest I had imagined, he didn't have a long beard or wear a black robe either.

I told him about my book. He was willing to take a chapter home with him and to give me his thoughts on my work. He then asked me to come to his church so that I could hear one of his messages. That was fair enough. Before leaving that day, he asked, "What made you include God in this book?"

"I don't know. Maybe it's because I can't get Him out of my mind," I replied.

George smiled, "Well, if you come to my church you'll probably learn some things about Him."

"I'd like that."

A couple of weeks later my girlfriend and I visited George's church. We both liked it. I went once more by myself, shortly before Christmas, and saw people being baptized. This was very moving. People shared gripping stories about their lives before they met Jesus. The changes in their lives because of meeting Him were amazing. One person talked about cheating on his wife and how this had devastated his family. He went on to talk about his guilt and how he felt trapped, thinking that there was no way out. Finally, he had confessed that he knew that this was wrong before God. God gave him the courage to confess this to his wife and to beg her for another chance. She forgave him and they started the work of marriage counseling. He went on to say he wanted to have a new life with Jesus.

That entire month (January 2002), George's church, West End Christian Community, was open to the public every evening. One of my sisters also attended this church. Her example gave me courage to go there. Although I attended church almost every day during that time, I slowly eased up in my searching for God. I suspected that I had done too many wrongs for God to ever forgive me. I felt I was not like these people—their problems seemed minor in comparison to what I had been through. Plus, my girlfriend was uncomfortable with all the time I was spending at this church. I thought I should just leave.

The final Sunday service of that month they had a guest speaker, a pastor who was supposedly a prophet. He came "to give the church a word," whatever that meant. For some reason, I ended up sitting in the front row. I spotted the guest speaking with my cousin George, and noticed an accent that hinted at Irish or English roots. That did nothing to dispel my expectation that it was going to be one boring message.

When he started, he quoted 1 Corinthians 15:33-34, which says, "Do not be misled: 'Bad company corrupts good character.' Come back to your senses as you ought, and stop sinning; for there are some who are ignorant of God—I say this to your shame." I slumped lower in my chair. I desperately wanted to get out of the church, but I couldn't because I was sitting in the front row. Those words pierced my heart. I finally recognized my lack of understanding of God. I didn't know Him at all, and I decided it had lots to do with all the bad company I had surrounded myself with.

People were invited to stay after the meeting to experience personal prayers and learn how to know God for themselves. I got up and went to stand in front of the speaker. He asked what I wanted prayer for.

"I'm an unrighteous man." I faltered, as tears streamed down my face.

"Why would you say such a thing?" he asked.

"I can't forgive myself for all the wrongs I have done and I don't see how can God forgive me."

He placed his hand on my head and began to pray something like this, "Lord you have heard this man's cry for forgiveness. Father, I pray the oil of gladness from your throne will pour down on this man's spirit as he receives your grace."

His hand on my head was like an anointing of that oil, and I could feel my hard heart beginning to crack open. Tears kept coming, and I knew something was changing inside me. I truly received forgiveness in my heart that day. Unlike the criminal justice system where a person's police record remains for their entire life, Jesus automatically gave me a pardon when I surrendered my life to Him.

When I went home and told my girlfriend what had happened, she seemed confused and troubled. She looked at me like I was crazy. She wasn't the only one. In fact, every time I shared with my family something I had read in the Bible or what God was showing me, someone would let me know they thought I was going nuts. My sister continued to support me, but it still wasn't easy. This type of rejection and abandonment felt even worse than what I had experienced when I went to prison.

chapter eleven

A Lonely Life

I stopped doing drugs. I gave up womanizing. Brawling, smoking, drinking, and cussing became things of the past. The people around me were freaking out at all these extreme changes. This hurt me a lot. I thought people would be happy that I was no longer the mean-spirited, selfish person I once was, but I was wrong. They mistook my good intentions to live out my faith and assumed I thought I was better than them.

I felt that God was asking me to be baptized and so I talked to my cousin George, the pastor, about this. He explained that my Greek baptism as a baby was my parents' decision for my life. It was their way of showing they wanted me to honor God and my Greek heritage. Now I wanted to obey Jesus' command to be baptized as a public testimony of my new life in Him. My cousin went on to explain that if God is asking you to do something, you should pay close attention and follow His ways.

The next day an alarming thought came to my mind. *You walked out of a crazy lifestyle that involved dangerous people—your family's life is in danger!* Fear seized me. Just when I had determined to obey God no matter what happened, my faith was being tested in a way I had not anticipated. For the first time, I used my Bible to help me through a dilemma. I randomly opened my Bible, hoping to receive an answer. My eyes focused on Proverbs 16:7: "When a man's ways please the Lord, He makes even his enemies to be at peace with him." This settled my heart. "Okay God…I'll trust you," I whispered.

My baptism was planned for the following month. To my great surprise, my cousin Demetre (Pastor George's brother) built up the courage to do the same thing. An even bigger surprise was that my girlfriend decided to be baptized, too. My family was greatly offended at my choice and my friends thought this was all too weird. They believed that I was denying my Greek Orthodox religion but really, I had never even practiced it. I respect those who follow it, but it did not satisfy my yearning for a personal relationship with God, although I do think that my religious background helped me to see my need for God.

The week before my baptism I heard God say, "Be at peace with your father and forgive him." It sounds ridiculous now, but I was angry to hear such things from God. I was just beginning to learn what obedience to God really means. The more I tried to convince myself that God would never ask me to do a thing like that, the more I was convinced it had to be done quickly. I finally built up enough nerve one day to approach my father to ask for his forgiveness. I still wanted to tell him about all his wrongs and the hurts he had brought into my life. In fact, I think I wrote a list of all his offenses, so that I wouldn't forget to mention a single one before I forgave him. It was a vengeful kind of record-keeping. Now I can see that my idea of forgiveness wasn't exactly lining up with what God wanted, but at least I was learning.

The day I met with my father, I looked into his eyes. To my surprise, I saw him as a little boy who had had a tough life of his own. I felt compassion for him. My hate for him was replaced by longing for what could have been. I wanted to hug him. I felt like I was a little boy again, too, wanting him to be my protective Daddy again. I began by saying something like this, "Dad, I know that I disappointed you lots and brought you great hurt. I have hated myself for years for hitting you when I was a rebellious teenager. I don't know why we ended up this way, but I don't want you to hate me anymore. I'm sorry that I shamed you and Mom by going to jail. I'm sorry for all the times I swore at you and disrespected your authority over my life. I know that you don't understand my life right now and why I'm going to church and following Jesus. I hope one day you can forgive me for being such a disappointment to you." I hung my head as sobs shook my frame. My tears fell faster than I could wipe them away.

My father started to cry with me. He wrapped his arms around me, kissing my cheeks. "Stop…Stop talking like this. I love you son. I love you. All I want is for you to be happy."

His actions said that he forgave me. My list of his offenses was not necessary. I was being healed and so was my father. There was no more calling him Andy; he became my father and my friend again.

God also asked me to stop the lawsuit that I had started against that shady landlord who had made me lose my restaurant. I felt relieved not having to deal with that anymore. I even forgave the Greek community I had blamed for lots of my family's misfortunes. (In fact, today God has given me a heart to love and a longing to minister to the Greek community of Winnipeg one day. I don't know what that will look like, but I continue to pray and wait for doors to be opened.)

Later that summer I became engaged to my girlfriend. Her parents had a Roman Catholic background, and thought that my passion and ideas about following Jesus were too weird. They kept meddling in our plans to get married, threatening that her family would reject her if she did not call off the wedding. In the fall, she caved in to their pressure. One day while I was at work, they came to our place, loaded up all her stuff, and got her to move somewhere else. I came home to an apartment that had been emptied of all evidence of our hopes. A note on the stove explained that our engagement was off.

Once again, I had to decide whether I would trust God for all my needs.

chapter twelve

wanting to win

My life became really hard. Even though my family felt sorry for me, they couldn't really understand, and they couldn't make things better for me. A few days after our breakup, I went to my girlfriend's workplace and asked her to talk to me. She begged me to leave the church and to stop being such a crazy Jesus fanatic. She told me that if I loved her, I would comply with her wishes. According to her, things needed to go back to the way they had been before my encounter with God, because, she maintained, we had been happier then. This was all too heavy for me to bear. I felt like I had driven her away from God. Feeling guilty, I complied with her conditions, but getting back together with her helped me face reality. I realized that she was not enough to keep me happy for the rest of my life. Being with her those few weeks I felt like I was betraying Jesus. That was far worse than losing a girlfriend. Finally, I called off our relationship. I should have been happy, but I wasn't.

I was still so miserable that sometimes I questioned whether I had done the right thing. As time went on being single was less and less fun. Often, I told Christians what I thought was the right thing to say—that God was enough for me—but that was a lie. I was not satisfied.

During that first year being alone, I shared my experiences with God with many people whenever I had a chance. It was strange that they listened to what I had to say about God. As I spent more time with other Christians, I had opportunity to see God working in many ways. I saw people being healed of anything from simple headaches to cancer-related diseases through the power of prayer. When my family heard that I was talking to strangers about God, they became worried that I was imposing my will on them. They misunderstood my motives; not realizing what I did was out of love for God and for other people. Even other people outside my family who were once close to me thought that my new life was strange.

I am thankful that my mother was very happy for me and encouraged me to keep doing God's will. I was also blessed in that two pastors mentored me. One was my cousin George and the other was Clint Toews, who is a spiritual father figure to me.

June 2004 was a great time in my parents' household because the Euro Cup of soccer was on and Team Greece had qualified. The Greek team's chances to win the entire tournament were a long shot—the odds against them were something like 250:1. Nobody was expecting them to score even a single goal but in their opening game they scored two goals and beat the host country, Portugal, 2-1. There were more high-fives and hugs in our household than we had ever seen. My mother really got into the spirit of the games just like the rest of us. She made us all laugh with her commentary on each of Greece's matches.

Dad kept making bets with people that Greece would lose every game. It was funny to watch him cheer for Greece even though he was losing money.

But at the same time as we were enjoying the soccer, we were struggling as a family, knowing that my father's health had taken a turn for the worse. He had become very weak and it seemed he had lost his will to live.

About a week into the tournament, my father asked me to give him a ride to his brother's place to watch Greece play against France. During that ride, I asked him if I could pray for him. He said, "No, I don't need anything. All I want, son, is for you to get married and have children."

"Okay, I'll do that, but you're going to have to ask God to bring a wife to me."

"Ask God for your wife?" He wasn't sure what to make of that.

"Yes, and while you're doing that agree with me in prayer that God will make you well so you can live to see that day."

Dad smiled, "Go ahead and pray, son."

The next day, Dad went to see his doctor and found out that he had a thyroid problem that could be easily corrected. Within a couple of weeks, he had regained strength and his desire to live returned. We were very glad. Once again, we enjoyed the excitement of soccer, especially as Greece headed into the final game against Portugal, this time for the prized Euro Cup. Dad was especially focused on the event. Our family gathered with many others in the Greek Orthodox Church basement where loyal Greeks cheered for their team. The game was intense. There was such great agony as each team had chances to score their first goal. I was so proud to be Greek but even prouder to be with my father to experience this once-in-a-lifetime game.

In the final minutes, Greece scored, thanks to a corner kick that got headed into the Portuguese net. The entire basement erupted in a noisy celebration. Tears shone on almost everyone's face. People hugged each other, sang and danced with as much gusto as if they had scored the goal themselves. My father lost another bet. I remember him saying to me, "If I was a truly patriotic… If I had put a thousand dollars on Greece when their odds were 250:1, I would have a quarter-million dollars right now."

Boy, did I laugh. "You are not meant to be a gambler, Dad," I said.

To this he replied, "No, but I am Greek."

chapter thirteen

Family Fun

One thing that I love about my dad is his odd sense of humor. Dad tells the funniest stories; what makes them funny is that he does not see the humor in them. He gets really worked up and excited. My favorite story is, 'The Guy in the Coffin'.

To imagine Dad entertaining us, it might help to picture a short Greek man with a heavy Greek accent, waving his big hands and pacing back and forth while he starts:

"Nobody has more bad luck than me! Before I got married, my brother Angelo and I shared a small apartment in Athens, Greece. One day my brother sends me downstairs to the landlord's apartment to pay the rent. I knock on the door and hear a voice say, 'Embros.' Turning the doorknob, I push and the door creaks open but nobody is there. No furniture except a coffin propped up on wheels in the middle of the living room. Strange, I think.

"Next thing you know this guy pops up from the coffin saying, 'Leave the money on the fridge.' I run so fast—right out of my building and for at least another half kilometer. The guy in the coffin was the landlord. What kind of a goof sleeps in a coffin?"

This is where most people start laughing, picturing my father running down a busy street in Athens in white-faced terror.

"What's so funny?" Father will interrupt, indignant that no one has sympathy for him.

So, he continues: "My story is not over! After I got married my wife and I moved to Winnipeg, Canada. Vasili was born and we lived downtown in a one-bedroom apartment near Central Park. One day I'm going out for a walk. While walking down my stairs, who do I see? The guy in the coffin from Athens, Greece followed me not only to Canada but Winnipeg, not only to Winnipeg but to Central Park! One in a billion chance that the guy in the coffin shows up here in my building!"

People usually are laughing hysterically while my father remains silent, not finding any of this humorous. "I'm not done!" Dad continues, mildly offended. "I see him coming up the stairs while I'm walking down. He looks up, only to find my boot in his face as he rolls to the bottom of the steps. Then I start yelling, 'Die, Dracula! Die!'"

Of course, the guy in the coffin did not die but my father thinks that was the worst strain of luck in his life. All of his stories contain some far-fetched elements.

Greeks love weddings. My family is no exception, and this is another part of my heritage that I cherish. One wedding that will always stand out in my memory took place a month before I met my now-wife. A guy I had known from my childhood was getting married to an Argentinean woman. At the reception, they served free alcohol. I was still single and my loneliness seemed sharper than ever when I saw others, like the newlyweds, so happy together. People were laughing and dancing. It seemed like almost everyone was having fun, including my six-year-old nephew, who stole the show with all his animated dancing.

Beginning to feel sad and out of place I started drinking alcohol. It was one way I could fit in with my family and friends and that felt good. After three drinks, my mood started to change for the better. When I started telling jokes and funny stories, I had the attention of my family and friends. Their outbursts of laughter encouraged me to continue. Dad joined in with his hilarious stories while I kept going back to the bar for more drinks. I was having a blast, making toasts drinking and recalling more funny stories that had happened to me.

Then one of the Greek ladies from my church approached me, asking how many drinks I had had.

"Why do you care?" I scoffed.

"Because you are not called to be like them! I am so ashamed of you right now. Put that drink away!" she added before she walked away.

I was fuming mad. *Who does she think she is to confront me that way? How dare she tell me that drinking is a sin?* I went back to the bar and asked for a triple rye and 7-Up with ice in a lowball glass. That used to be my favorite drink before I quit getting drunk in 2001.

I looked onto the dance floor and saw my little nephew pretending to be drunk like most of the folks who were dancing. Suddenly, the fun was over. I felt sad all over again and wanted to cry. Just as my little nephew came toward me, he began to vomit all over himself.

I slammed my drink onto the bar and ran towards him. His parents got to him first and cleaned him up as well as they could. This took away all my desire to party. My mother noticed my sadness and asked me if I was all right.

"I'm going home," I replied. I left the wedding and I walked away from my old life.

chapter fourteen

Finding Acceptance

I had moved back into my parents' home in order to clean up my life and to save money after the break-up with my fiancée. One night I poured out to God my displeasure about being single. Falling silent, I contemplated the kind of character I would like to see in my future wife. I imagined a life partner who would be gentle, honest, wise, self-controlled, pure, affectionate, respectful, meek, humble and very soft-spoken.

Not long after that I met up with a very good friend whom I used to meet to pray for the men in our church. He started to tell me his issues between him and his girlfriend's roommate. As I listened to him complain about her, I asked him if she was single.

"Did you not hear a word that I said to you about her?" he asked.

"I did. I want to meet this so-called traditional Christian girl you're telling me about."

"Why?" He seemed confused.

As he told me about her principles, faith and love for God's Word, my spirit leaped for joy. She sounded very much like the person I had asked God for. I turned to my friend and said, "Set up a double date with her or invite a bunch of friends for all of us to go out somewhere."

He walked away, laughing and shaking his head. "I'll call you later this week and let you know."

I waved goodbye to him as he drove away in his truck. Later that week he called me to tell me the young woman was out of the country at a friend's wedding. Doubts began to trouble me. *Well, maybe it wasn't meant to be.* A couple of weeks later my friend called, asking if I was still interested in meeting his girlfriend's roommate. I told him I was and, not long after, a group of us met at the Greek Orthodox Church for a folk culture event. I arrived late and I was nervous. When I sat down at the table, everyone else was already eating.

My friend introduced my date. "Billy, meet Trudy," he said, indicating the young woman I'd been waiting to meet.

I realized I had briefly been introduced to her the year before but we had never talked. She was beautiful. I took in her great smile, her pretty blue eyes and fantastic laugh. It was hard to talk with so much commotion going on, but I just knew I wanted to spend more time with her. We went to a few more gatherings but I was looking for an opportunity to know more about this beautiful person.

It happened in a unique way. My friend and I offered to throw a barbecue at the girls' place. As I followed everyone up the stairs, carrying a large shallow pan with all our barbecued meat, I tipped the pan a little and suddenly hot oil and meat juice ran all the way down my legs. The heat of my embarrassment was as uncomfortable as the spilled juices soaking my pants.

"I have to go home," I said.

The others looked back and saw the mess. I could tell they were as embarrassed as I was.

"I'll be back soon." I assured them.

"Don't be silly. I'll go to my brother's place down the street to get you a pair of his pants," Trudy offered.

Reluctantly, I agreed. When she came back she brought me a pair of sweat pants that were a little short. I felt dumb wearing sweat pants with a dress shirt and dress socks. Though I tried to be a good sport about it, I really wanted to go home and change after we were all done eating.

"I'll be back," I said and stood up.

"Take Trudy with you." her roommate suggested.

Trudy looked uncomfortable and I felt awkward too. "I'll be back soon," I insisted.

Trudy glared at her friend who was insisting that we leave together.

"All right, let's go, Trudy," I said.

We walked to my car and I opened the door for her. When I sat down, I blurted out, "Trudy, I've been wondering about how to tell you stuff about myself because, frankly, it's not very good. There's so much to tell that I don't know where to begin. I guess the best thing for me is to jump right in. I have a beautiful daughter, Ashley. I haven't seen her in nine years. I don't have visiting rights so I don't know if she'll even want to see me when she gets to the stage where she needs to get some answers. Also, many years ago, I spent some time in prison for drug trafficking. So, if you're not interested in me, I'll leave on my own."

Trudy smiled, "Well, that's who you used to be. That's not who you are now. Jesus has forgiven your past. Who am I to judge you for it? And yes, I'm interested in getting to know you better."

I could hardly believe my ears. Words couldn't express my gratitude, and I'm sure I kept smiling the rest of the evening. That evening was the beginning of the most wonderful part of my life. I wondered why I hadn't paid more attention to this young woman the first time I saw her. I had promised my friend I would drop off a disc for his girlfriend, Trudy's roommate. Trudy had walked by as I stood in the doorway and we were quickly introduced. I found out later in our courtship that Trudy was not feeling well that day, and that's why she paid no attention to me.

Now I was pretty sure my prayer for a godly wife was about to be answered and there was no way I was going to do anything to jeopardize this exciting prospect. During our courtship, I asked the Lord to keep us pure and to give me the strength to resist temptations.

We spent hours walking and talking about our dreams and hopes. We often went out for coffee. I think we visited every Tim Horton's in Winnipeg, sometimes even going to three different Timmys in one night. We both agreed on a desire to have children. I often led our conversations by letting her know how things were going between us. I made it clear from the start that my aim in getting to know her was with the intention of marriage. I remember asking her, after courting her for two months, if I could hold her hand. Eleven days later, on Remembrance Day, as we walked along the river in a quaint little neighborhood in old St. Boniface, I first told Trudy that I loved her.

We did break up for almost a week. There was a huge misunderstanding on both our parts. Trudy was the acting administrator for the church at the time, and felt very stressed out. She was very busy doing year-end and we barely saw each other for a couple of weeks. One night we were talking on the phone and I had to hang up without much warning, I think because my father needed the phone for a few minutes. I told Trudy I would call her back when he was done. I called her back a few minutes later only to get her answering machine. I left a message but she did not get back to me until the following day. By then I had assumed that she was no longer interested in me. She, on the other hand, did not hear the phone, and thought it was strange that I did not call her back. The next day she heard the message and tried to call me. But I did not take or return any of her many phone calls. I was obviously hurt and did not handle things well.

Several days later, my friend talked to me in church. He told me I was being immature. He said that the least I could do was to hear her out. I was annoyed with my friend but deep inside, I knew that he was right. I told my friend to tell her that if she wanted to call me she could. We agreed to meet and talk over coffee.

I arrived at the coffee shop first and waited for her. I tried to prepare myself to be tough because I fully intended to tell her face-to-face that our relationship was not going to work out.

But when I saw her, she had a special glow about her. She sat down at the table and asked if I would like to lead the conversation. I refused, so she started to talk. She explained what had happened. The next thing I knew, as I stared into her beautiful blue eyes, I realized this truly was the woman I wanted to marry. Trudy asked me a couple of times if I was even hearing a single word that she said, because I just kept smiling at her. I guess she could see that I was smitten! I told her that I had missed her and that I still loved her. From that day on I committed myself to this beautiful woman and vowed I would do everything to fight for our relationship.

I had asked Trudy's father for her hand but instead, he told me to ask her pastor's advice. I told him that I was committed to marrying her. I told him I really wanted to leave with his blessing, but he chose not to give me his answer. (Now I realize Trudy's father finds it hard to talk about things that are close to his heart. I have learned over the years that Trudy's father demonstrates love more by helping than with words. I love him more than ever and appreciate him for raising Trudy to know and love the Lord, and for giving me a wonderful mate for life.)

That same day I told my father of my intentions to marry Trudy, and he was so proud to give me his blessing. The next day, May 31, 2005 I took Trudy down Memory Lane. We went full circle to all the places where significant events of our relationship had occurred.

I took her for a ride over our favorite bridge and squeezed her hand. We went to the place where I first asked to hold her hand. Then we went to one of our favorite Greek restaurants. There Trudy told me, "I don't think it would be a big deal if we had our first kiss on the day we get engaged."

I quickly replied, "That's not likely to happen because we have come this far, and I made a promise to God that I would not do something that might get me into trouble. I want to honor that promise to Him and you."

Trudy smiled. I could see she understood my concern for both of us. With God's help, I kept my word to Him and Trudy until our wedding day.

After supper, I got very nervous because I suspected Trudy sensed this was the day I was going to propose. We went for a walk in our favorite part of St. Boniface and I stopped at the exact spot I had first told her I loved her. Finally, we drove toward the Greek Orthodox Church where we had had our first date, but I tried to choose a route that would not give away our destination.

As we walked towards the church, Trudy commented, "Isn't the Greek church in this area?" I was breathing deeply, trying to calm myself. Trudy is so observant! She asked if I was okay. I ignored her, not wanting to lose the courage to ask her to marry me. When we got to the front courtyard, I asked her to sit on a bench in that beautiful area with its gated doors.

I was distracted for a moment as I looked at the area where, ten years earlier, I had heard those Greek men commenting on my reputation.

"That was long ago." Trudy had caught my glance; she knew the story.

"I know. That was a very painful moment in my life and I want to replace it with something better."

I knelt in front of Trudy. I told her how much I loved her and asked if she would honor me by marrying me. I presented her with an unset diamond because I wanted her to design a band that she would cherish for the rest of her life. We hugged and she said, "Yes, I'll marry you! I love you too."

I could barely contain my joy. I felt like shouting the good news to anyone who would listen! I marveled at how God was putting my broken past on a new foundation. I was at peace, even though I struggled with issues of past pain and insecurity. I would be marrying the woman of my dreams and looked forward to building a new life with her. That was something I had longed for so long. Even though this was a huge, clean "high," there were more lessons of restoration to come.

chapter fifteen

Back to Wellington

Some of the lessons I was learning meant revisiting the past. It was 2005, a few months before I got married and I was still living at home. One day my brother needed a ride to work. As we were driving down Wellington Avenue, where all my siblings and I walked when we went to Wellington Elementary School, he pointed out the slum-like conditions of our neighborhood.

My brother kept observing the teenage prostitutes and the gangsters that were controlling them. "How can anyone stand watching this?" he agonized. "We didn't have to see this crap as kids, and no kid on the way to school should have to see it."

I nodded.

"Why don't you do something about this?" he challenged.

"Like what? Our Member of the Legislature knows they are walking up and down the street not too far from his office, and it doesn't seem to bother him."

"Politicians don't give a rip about this area! This needs to stop."

"I know…but what can I do?"

"This is sickening. I hate driving down this street. Used needles are lying on the sidewalks; used condoms and broken beer bottles litter our back lanes. Gang logos are spray-painted on people's houses, and vandalized vehicles are everywhere. Crack houses can be found on every block, and there are far too many teenage girls, even little girls on crack selling their bodies—and for what?"

The sad evidence of our community falling apart was heavy on both our hearts, but I felt helpless. We were almost at my brother's workplace. "Do you even care?" he asked me one last time before he exited the car.

"What do you want me to do? Follow these girls to see where they get their crack cocaine? Maybe I should beat up their pimps! I see and I pray, but God hasn't done anything yet!"

"God? Why not you?"

I stopped and rolled down my window as my brother walked away from the car. "I do care… I guess I don't think there is much I can do."

My brother gave me a half-smile, "Thanks for the ride." He hesitated only a moment. "I just hate the way things have become."

"Me too." I smiled back and he walked on to begin his day at work.

I drove back towards Wellington Avenue but then, on impulse, I made a right turn and headed for my elementary school. As I opened the front door, I got a whiff of books and sweaty runners, chalk and lunchroom aromas, and it brought back all the memories of my early years in school. Everything became familiar. Children crossed in front of my path, and my heart started to weep. I went straight for the offices and asked for the principal.

"Whom shall I say you are?" the receptionist asked.

"I'm a former student. I walked up and down these halls twenty-three years ago. My name is Billy Vassilopoulos."

She spoke briefly with someone on the telephone, and a person came to greet me. "I'm the vice principal," the lady said, introducing herself.

"I would like a moment to talk to you in private concerning illegal activities happening where the children walk to school."

"Come to my office," she responded, and I followed. "Our hands are tied, Mr. Vassilopoulos, if you're inquiring about the drug dealers and prostitutes in this area."

"What do you mean? Are you saying you haven't called the police?"

"The police can only get involved if a parent like you makes a complaint. But their hands are tied as well. They'll patrol the area for a couple of days just to make the drug dealers uneasy, and this will cause the prostitutes to move to a different street, but they'll be back by next week."

"You've got to be kidding me."

"I'm afraid I'm not. The problem is there are not enough parents who care like you do right now to make a difference in this area. What grade is your child in?"

"I don't have a child in this school."

"Then why are you here?"

"This is my old school. This is my old neighborhood."

"I imagine it has changed a lot since you came here."

"Yeah, but for the worse."

She folded her hands on her desk, and smiled ruefully at me.

I stood up, "I guess there's nothing I can do?"

"Oh, but there is. You figure out a way to get into the legal system and you'll make a difference one day. You have a heart for this community," she replied.

I shook her hand and thanked her for her time. The next day I drove my brother to work again. This time there were no prostitutes and no gangsters down Wellington Avenue. We spotted a couple of police vehicles.

"Well, it's about time," my brother commented.

"Yeah, but this won't last long," I replied.

"How do you know?" he asked.

"I felt helpless after I talked to you. Out of desperation, I guess, I went to our old school."

"And?"

I explained everything to him and he smiled at me. "But it's a start. They will have to take you seriously the next time you talk to them."

"I don't think there will be a next time. I'm not cut out for this stuff."

"What? Are you kidding me? You're an ex-criminal who has changed his life around. You have a good reputation now and people will listen to someone like you. You can't stop now."

"Maybe one day, but not now," I replied, still feeling overwhelmed.

"Don't keep looking at yourself as someone people won't listen to. You have a lot to offer now. You're a new man."

I was amazed to hear how much confidence my brother had in me. I dropped the conversation that day, but this is still a burning issue in my heart.

chapter sixteen

It's Not Easy

M y new life required that I look for honest work instead of searching for an easy way to make a buck, so early that May I took a job with a family-run company called Under the Sun Enterprises, Incorporated.

At first, I had thought it was a crazy idea when Trudy suggested applying to that company but after some thought I considered at least going for a job interview. During my interview, I quickly realized I had no skills related to building electrical fences for livestock. In fact, I had no idea what the rancher, Peter, was talking about. I told him that I didn't even know how to swing a hammer properly to set fence posts, or the names of certain tools. I was amazed that he wasn't fazed by my inexperience. He asked me about my relationship with my father and I told him how God had restored it. That satisfied him and the following month I was off to work with him.

Every day was a challenge, but I persevered. I must have helped this poor man's patience level go up a few notches.

One of my jobs was feeding his horses and cleaning the stalls before we headed off to our job sites. I was terrified of his horses, but over time I overcame that fear. My boss was an untiring worker. It was a tough summer for his business since it rained almost every day, often leaving me without work and him without an income.

I will never forget a particular dairy farm. We began re-wiring one fence when a herd of cows began to head our way. A couple of times, I caught sight of huge horns and then discovered that the large horns belonged to a massive specimen of a bull. I told my boss there was a bull heading our way but he told me to stop exaggerating and to keep working. The herd parted, revealing the bull. Again, I told Peter, but he got angry with me. Then he looked up. "Oh my God there's a bull!" he mumbled, dumbfounded.

"What do we do?" I asked, afraid I wouldn't make it to our wedding.

"Just ignore him and keep working," he replied.

I was mentally planning my escape route as the bull got closer. *This job doesn't pay me enough to deal with this madness!* By now the great threatening beast was within two feet of my boss and five feet away from me.

My boss reached out his hand and scratched the bull's head, saying, "What's the matter, huh?"

The bull seemed annoyed, but then turned around and walked the other way. I saw that I had exaggerated the entire situation. I was obviously not an animal man.

After work, we walked by the barn where we met the owner of the dairy operation. "Done for the day?" he asked.

"Hey, you have a loose bull in that field with your herd of cows," my boss told the owner.

"Are you guys all right?" he asked. "That bull has attacked two of my hired men in the last couple of months. One of them is still in the hospital recovering."

I had a hard time sleeping that night. I dreaded going back to that same worksite. But sure enough, the following morning we drove back there. Peter told me to measure up the length of a field nearby. We went in different directions, and guess who came to visit me before long? Yes, the slobbering, crazy bull. It didn't help that it was very windy and that my boss was far away. I kept calling out Peter's name but the wind swallowed the sound of my voice. The only thing between me and the crazy bull was the pile of seven-foot posts we were using for our fences.

The bull chased me around the pile. He wouldn't head over the pile but he kept trying to sweep away some of the posts as he pawed on the ground to intimidate me.

I'm not dying this way! I said to myself, picking up one of the posts. I kept swinging it, threatening to hit him, but he wasn't afraid of me. I couldn't run away because the field was too large. It seemed my boss was indifferent because he kept walking without looking back. I was on my own. It was just me and a crazed bull. I was convinced he was intent on killing me. His nostrils flared as he shook his head. Seeing that huge tongue flopping around in the wind once again really unnerved me.

I had had enough. I swung the post as hard as I could. This made a loud thump sound, but the bull didn't flinch. I reached to pick up another post to strike him. To my relief, he began kicking his feet high into the air and took off the other way. When my boss came back, I told him what had happened. He laughed, "Good for you. Let's get back to work."

That angry bull seemed to represent the worst that life could bring to me. In the face of danger, I had carried on. A new confidence rose up in me to be able to face the future with God in charge of my life.

chapter seventeen

Finding Family

We got married fifteen months after Trudy said she was interested in getting to know me. My brother was my best man, and one of Trudy's closest friends served as her maid of honor. We wore the traditional Greek white crowns, tied together to symbolize unity. We had a candle-light evening wedding like they do in Argentina. My cousin George and John Mickelfield officiated. Five other pastors joined them towards the end of our ceremony and offered prayers for us. Without consciously planning it, we had seven ministers just as my parents had had seven priests at their wedding. But, our wedding was different from a traditional Greek wedding in some ways. There, the bride and groom do not speak, and they do not kiss. We said our personal vows, and on the day of our wedding in November, we could finally share our first kiss.

We went to a local resort for three days for our first honeymoon and shortly after that we travelled to Argentina for our second honeymoon. There, Trudy's wonderful family was awaiting our arrival. We rented a chalet in the town where Trudy had grown up. That gave us a chance to spend time with her family.

I loved meeting all my new aunts, uncles, nieces and nephews. Though we had a language barrier, they embraced me as one of their own. My brother-in-law John had bragged about the amazing beef in Argentina. "The steaks are so tender that you can scoop them with a spoon," he would say. When I got the first chance to have my first steak, I was sold. It was the best steak I had ever eaten. There, barbecuing is quite an art, and I loved practicing it on the family.

I promised the kids that I would make them my famous pizzeria-style pizza. Many of Trudy's family members enjoyed the pizza, and urged me to open a pizzeria in their town. Listening to their voices made it a little easier, at least for a while, to ignore a call from God. I had sensed He was asking me to serve him as a pastor in a church one day. This burning feeling in a man's heart and spirit is hard to get rid of; I had felt it a few times before.

The time flew by quickly and when we landed back in Winnipeg after five weeks, it was shocking to feel the cold again. I wondered if this was how my parents had felt about leaving their warm country when they arrived in Manitoba.

Within seven months of our return, we opened a pizzeria in the Elmwood area of Winnipeg. I had defaulted to something that I was comfortable with instead of answering God's call. I was scared. I was convinced my terrible past disqualified me from serving God as a pastor. I tried reasoning with myself about it in that way, because I wished this notion of a calling would go away and leave me alone.

During our first year of operation Vasilly's Pizzeria showed promise but shortly after that, we could no longer afford to pay our rent at home if the business was going to survive. Then the sudden recession shook our business. We made the difficult decision to give up the home we were renting. That meant we would stay at Aunt Maria and Uncle Christo's home on weekdays and with my in-laws on the weekends. The transition was harder for me than for Trudy but we managed to make it work.

My aunt and uncle were so much fun. "You're not leaving us until there's a baby on the way," my aunt teased.

Trudy became pregnant in 2008. The night when she did a home pregnancy test, confirming our suspicions, there were no words to describe the joy in my heart. Filled with excitement, I couldn't sleep for two days. Our parents were thrilled with our news.

"We have to move," I told my aunt.

"Why? Don't you like living with us?"

"We will be moving in with my in-laws for a while."

"What about us?"

"You told me once that if there was a baby on the way, we could leave your home."

Tears welled up in Aunt Maria's eyes. "I had a dream last week that Trudy was holding a baby girl." She smiled and touched Trudy's stomach.

"Thank you for everything you and Uncle have done for us. I don't know how we could ever repay you."

"You already have with this wonderful news. We are so happy for you!" Her excitement was easy to see.

Three days after we'd shared our news, Trudy started having complications that brought us to the Emergency Room. The doctor told us that Trudy was losing the baby but the good news was we could try again in a few months.

"I don't accept that!" I snapped.

"Tomorrow I'll send her for an ultrasound to confirm it," the doctor replied.

Dumbfounded by her cold-heartedness, I took my wife's hand and smiled. "Well, like I said, I don't accept what you're saying." I reiterated as we prepared to leave.

That night we called people to join us in prayer. We prayed hard, grieved deeply and dreamed cautiously. Pregnancy opens up a whole new world, but it was a world we knew only God could open to us.

At the ultrasound appointment, I was not allowed to join Trudy. The clinic staff told me that they would call me in forty-five minutes to find out the results. During this time, I was uneasy but somehow, I found strength in God. I felt His closeness and His comfort during the longest waiting time of my life. Even time in jail seemed short by comparison. Maybe it was because the lives of the two people I cared most about were hanging in the balance. I had read in a pregnancy book that just six weeks after life begins, a fluttering heartbeat could be seen on an ultrasound. "Lord, let us see that fluttering heart," I prayed.

The ultrasound technician came to get me. When I entered the room, my wife had tears in her eyes.

"Do you want to see your baby's heart?" the technician asked.

"Of course I do," I replied as I sat down, kissing Trudy's hand.

We had been given no hope at the hospital the night before but God had decided to give us the gift of life.

Trudy was not able to work with me at the pizzeria for a while but eventually she was allowed to return.

We now lived with Trudy's parents in Landmark, Manitoba. The commute from there to the pizzeria in Winnipeg was taking its toll on me. The stress of running a struggling business and worrying about how I was going to provide for our family was overwhelming, to say the least. But there was a lot of joy, too. Every week I read out of a pregnancy book about the stages of development a baby goes through. This brought great joy to my loving in-laws.

Throughout Trudy's pregnancy, my daughter Ashley kept coming to my mind. Ashley's eighteenth birthday was coming up that summer. I felt if Ashley were going to make an attempt to see me this would be the age at which she would try. A month before her birthday, she contacted my parents, making arrangements to see them. They were able to see her but she was not ready to meet me.

Ashley's mother called me a few weeks after Ashley's birthday, wanting to meet me because she had heard from my parents and siblings that I was a changed man. I met with her and owned up to my failures and the hurts that I had caused us all. She forgave me, and a couple of months later, I got the opportunity to see Ashley after an absence of thirteen years. We met at a park. It didn't go as I hoped. I wanted to hug her and never let her go again but all I got was a handshake from a beautiful but frightened young woman.

Anything I said fell on deaf ears. My explanations were ignored. She wanted nothing to do with me ever again. My absence in those early years had hurt her heart deeply. I could see it in her eyes. Time doesn't always heal old wounds and sometimes the scars left are too much to bear. I had dreaded the possibility that my daughter would not hear me out—and now my worst fear had come true.

When I returned home, Trudy saw the pain in my eyes. She continues to offer me so much support and care, and I am thankful to God for a godly wife who accepted me with my past, and with the pain that it brings. I still pray that someday Ashley and I will be able to reconcile, so that I can help her to learn about God's father-heart of love.

chapter eighteen

Heaven or Not

I learned that a former neighbor and an old family friend, was dying from complications associated with diabetes. I smiled as I thought of my early memories of this man. He had always managed to scare me half-to-death with his powerful voice. When I wasn't looking, he would shout out, "Billy!" I jumped every time.

He no longer frightened me. Many things were different now. He knew about my troubled past. I visited him in the hospital whenever I could escape from the demands of my restaurant. On one of my last visits I knew it wasn't going to be long before he would be gone forever. I was hesitant to talk to him about God, because he knew so much about me, but that day I felt that I needed to explain how my life had changed.

"Do you ever think about heaven?" I asked him as I sat down on the edge of his bed. I needed to be close so I could hear him, and I wanted him to sense my caring.

"Billy," he said softly. His voice crackled, "Who knows if there is a heaven, Billy?"

His wife sat on the other side of his bed, just listening.

"There's a story in the Bible that tells about a rich man who had plenty, and a poor beggar, Lazarus, who showed up at his door, desperate for food. Jesus told this story to describe the two differences between heaven and a place some call hell. Are you interested in hearing it?" I asked.

He nodded his head and I continued, "The day came when both men died. Angels carried Lazarus into heaven where there was great comfort and safety. The rich man found himself in a place of torment called Hades, or hell. The conditions were so terrible for the rich man that he begged Lazarus to dip his finger in his water cup to cool off his burning tongue. There was a great gap between them, not permitting any one from either side to visit the other. Abraham, who was with Lazarus in heaven, told the rich man that he had had his chance to do what was right while he lived on earth, but that he had ignored the poor and given his table scraps to the dogs while the poor man went hungry.

"The rich man, realizing that his five brothers were still living on earth, had the same attitude as he begged Abraham to warn his brothers not to end up where he was. Abraham told him, 'Your brothers have the words of Mosses and the prophets, but even if a man were to die and rise again from the dead your brothers would still not believe.'"

He looked at me with fear in his eyes, "Jesus told this story?"

"Yes. Time is not on your side, and you need to decide where you will wake up after you close your eyes for the last time."

"What do I have to do?"

"You have to understand that your ways and God's ways are not the same. Sin is going against God's wishes for your life. Just like the rich man in the story, your heart's attitude is what separates you from God. There is hope and peace for you now if you confess before God that you are a sinner. Admit that you need His forgiveness. That's how you can prevent an outcome like the rich man's."

A tear escaped and rolled down his cheek.

I asked, "Do you understand that you are a sinner?"

"Yes, I'm a sinner."

"That's good—you just apologized to God. Do you want to be forgiven from your sins?"

"Yes."

"Would you like for me to guide you in prayer so you can invite Jesus into your heart?"

"Yes."

I held his hand and looked into his eyes. I prayed, asking Jesus to fill his heart with God's love, and to let him realize that he and God were now at peace. I assured him that he did not need to fear dying anymore. We talked about making peace with his wife and children. He said something to his wife in Italian, but I didn't understand what he said. I told him to talk to his son about how much he loved him. He promised he would.

A month later he passed away. One of his daughters asked me to give a message on salvation in their Roman Catholic Church. She was concerned for those in her immediate family and other relatives who were not following Jesus. I was not comfortable with that because her brother and I did not see eye to eye. I was afraid that he would cause problems, and that was the last thing I wanted to do to her grieving family. She insisted that I speak, but I had a feeling that many of my former companions would be there. I could imagine they would be ready to judge me and might tell me off for leaving my old lifestyle and abandoning them. I told her I would think about it.

The next day she called me again. "Billy, I talked to the priest, and, as you predicted, he was not impressed to hear that you are going to speak at my father's funeral."

"I don't understand," I replied, feeling relieved that I did not have to speak.

"I told the priest that you are a godly man and that you and my father talked about God before he died. The priest had the nerve to ask me how long you planned on talking. I told him I thought it could be ten to fifteen minutes, but he told me that you needed to restrict your talk to five minutes, because we don't want to hold the mourners captive with a long-winded message."

"Five minutes will be enough." I thought that would be easier for me.

"You speak whatever God puts on your heart and leave the timeline up to me!"

I didn't have a chance to respond before she hung up the phone.

The more I thought about it, the more apprehensive I became. Trudy kept assuring me that everything would be okay.

On the day of the funeral, she asked me if I had a word from the Bible for all the people in attendance. I told her that I did have a word, but I wasn't sure how the priest and the people would receive it.

"I asked the priest how much time I have to speak," she told me. "He told me I could take all the time I wanted." She smiled and amazed me with her resourcefulness. "I told him I was going to speak for twenty minutes, but I had decided to give my time to you instead."

"You told the priest that?"

"I did and you should have seen the look on his face." She laughed.

Trudy and I arrived at the church early. At first there were only a few people, but within a few minutes, more arrived, and then the church quickly filled to more than two hundred people. I was now very nervous. Some of my old partying friends were there and so were many people I had once hung around with. This was not good. I had my message on two pages of paper because I was afraid I was not going to be allowed to read out of my Bible.

The time arrived for me to speak. I stood at the pulpit, looking over all the faces staring at me. The sight of all those people who did not know God nearly broke my heart; I was no longer afraid of speaking in front of them.

I started off with a thunderous shout, "Eh, Billy!"—trying to mimic the way my old neighbour used to greet me. I talked about my last talk with him and the decision he had made to allow Jesus into his heart. I shared with his family the love he had for his wife and children, and my hope that he had taken the chance to make things right with them. There was complete silence in the church as I read the story of Lazarus and the rich man from the Gospel of Luke, verses nineteen to thirty-one of chapter sixteen. I described his longing to know if there was a heaven. I told the people that there is no such place as purgatory or any other temporary holding place for people to get their act together before they enter heaven. "Purgatory is here now, so make the decision now before you close your eyes for the last time."

I challenged the family and the entire gathering in that church not to wait until they found themselves on their deathbed, like my old neighbour did, to make the decision to know and follow Jesus. I acknowledged my own sinful past. I explained my gratitude for the opportunity to follow Jesus. I paused to look over the congregation. Almost every face was blank. I turned to gaze at his son. As I focused on his grief-weary face, I knew I had to make sure he knew that his father loved him deeply. I said it there, just in case my old neighbour had not gotten the chance to tell him.

"Eh, Billy!" I shouted one last time and then concluded, "I look forward to hearing my old neighbour call my name when I enter heaven one day." Before I walked off the stage, I gave the priest a friendly glance. I returned to my seat beside Trudy, and she squeezed my hand.

The last thing left to do was to shake the hands of the family members and to express our condolences. I was terrified to talk to his son, but when it was finally my turn to speak to him, he fell into my arms and we cried together. We didn't need words just then.

This experience was a real eye-opener. I realized I have an amazing opportunity to keep on serving as I continue praying for my old friends. I want to convey my love and God's love for them every chance I get.

chapter nineteen

Losses and Gains

People around us seemed oblivious to the state of our struggling business because I refused to allow business woes to steal my joy that I was going to be a father again soon.

One morning, Trudy wakened me at six-thirty. She touched my hand and lightly rubbed my face, saying, "I'm sorry to wake you, but I think it's time for us to head to the hospital."

My eyes struggled to open, "Are you saying it's time?" I mumbled.

Trudy smiled. "Let's get ready to go."

Trying to stay calm, I managed to get us to the city safely, driving as quickly as was prudent. We made it to the hospital around eight-thirty. All the beds in the maternity ward were full. Staff told us that they might have to send us to a different hospital.

"We are having our baby here!" I told the nurse.

Trudy added another argument. "But my doctor is here!"

"We will check you first and we will take it from there," the nurse replied calmly.

They checked Trudy and decided that she was too far along to transfer to another hospital. Six hours later our precious little girl Andigoni (Anna) Aurora was born. We named her after our mothers. The nurses passed her to me first. Seeing this tiny new person, all bundled up, made all my problems seem petty. A couple of days later we took her home. Trudy's parents were overjoyed to have their grand-daughter come live with them. A baby brings so much life into a home. Having little Anna in our room and knowing she was ours reminded us of God's goodness in our lives.

But being a father again brought back old insecurities. I wondered if I would do a good job raising Anna. My fear was that when troubles arose in her life I might not be there to protect her. My father always told me, "You never stop worrying about your children; it's just part of life." Now I could understand what he meant.

chapter twenty

Sharing the Profit

Through my pizzeria restaurant, I had many opportunities to encourage others to put their trust in God and to seek out a relationship with Him. Many times, we did so by handing out Bibles to those who showed an interest in our story. We also left free Bibles on a table for anyone who wanted one.

My heart went out to all the little children in the neighborhood who had no fathers in their lives. They loved visiting us. I would spin and toss pizza dough in the air as these little faces smiled at me. The children called me Mr. Vasilly and they called my wife Mrs. Vasilly. We often had meals with these little ones and prayed for them. Many people in our area knew we were religious. This must have kept us safe for the most part because crime kept escalating in the area as time passed.

Teenaged gangsters tried to claim our pizzeria business as their drug haven. They would sit in our restaurant while setting up drug deals on their cell phones in a code language.

Little did they know that I was familiar with all that from my past. Knowing what they were up to, I would walk out of the kitchen area and go sit out in the front of the restaurant where they were. I would choose a table next to the drug dealers and would open up a Bible. This made some of them feel extremely uncomfortable, causing them to leave. Others would ask, "What are you reading?"

I told them how they reminded me of myself as a teenager.

"How so?" they'd ask.

I took the opportunity to tell them my story about my past, especially my experience in prison. They were scared but intrigued. "Man, you know how hard it is to quit selling drugs. How did you get out of your gang and live to talk about it?"

A lot of these young boys and men listened to me when I talked to them about Jesus and how He had helped me walk away from my dangerous and crazy past.

One weekend that I'll never forget is when a scary-looking man came to our restaurant door late at night. We had closed the business and were ready to go home. Seeing us inside with the lights all off didn't persuade him to leave. He didn't seem to take notice we were not open. Trudy's friend was visiting us. Taking notice of her, he pounded on our glass door, pleading with me to sell him cold slices of pizza if I had any left. Feeling badly for him, I opened the door and followed him to the cashier counter. He started being very friendly with Trudy's friend who had Anna sitting on her lap. I signaled to Trudy to go get Anna.

"Cute baby," he said with a smile.

"My daughter," I replied, "Here are your pizza slices." I began punching in his order.

"Save your taxes. You don't have to punch it in for me," he commented with a smirk. He handed me a five-dollar bill.

I responded, "Next time if you come here and place an order you'll notice it will cost you more but since I don't have any money in the cash register to give you change I'll let it go this time."

"No money in the cash register?"

"Not a penny!" I smiled and he walked out of the restaurant.

A couple of days later he returned. There was nobody else in our restaurant. I greeted him with a hello which he ignored. He kept pacing in front of me as I stood behind the cash register. He looked nervous and very annoyed as he kept looking out the windows.

"What can I get for you?" I asked.

"Nothing! Why?" he muttered, continuing to pace back and forth in front of me.

"Are you waiting for somebody?"

"No."

"Are you thirsty?"

"I have no money."

"I'll buy you a soft drink," I replied. "What will it be?"

He pointed to his choice of drink in the glass front cooler. I handed it to him and he made his way over to one of the tables and sat down. I followed and sat across from him. We briefly stared at each other.

"How long have you been out of jail?" I asked.

Surprised at my question, he answered after taking a sip of his drink. "Two weeks…How did you know?"

"What are you doing to stay out of jail these days?"

"Just keeping low, but I've been offered jobs to make big money."

"Is it worth going back into prison?"

He laughed. "I could do the time standing on my head."

"Really? I didn't find prison that comfortable."

"What prison were you at, white boy?" he scoffed.

"Stony Mountain."

He smirked. "You were in the big house?"

"1995. Served time for drug trafficking."

"How many times you've been back?"

"None…thank God."

"How so?"

"Lots of luck in the beginning, but then I chose to follow Jesus."

"White man's religion. I tried Christianity in prison but it's all a hoax."

"What makes you say that?"

"I believe in a Creator."

"So do I."

"Not my Creator!"

"Probably not. Your Creator must be pretty weak if he can't keep you out of jail."

Glaring at me he guzzled the rest of his drink and slammed the can down on the table. "What's that supposed to mean?" he growled.

"You probably worship some sort of animal instead of the one who created that animal. To me that kind of religion seems backwards."

"Go on."

"The Christianity that you think is a hoax is the Christianity I found to be the only religion that I know where God will accept a person right where they are." Seeing that he was having a hard time following what I was trying to say, I tried again. "It means that a person doesn't have to get their act together before God can accept them for who they are. Do you remember the two thieves that hung on either side of Jesus when he was on the cross?"

"I have heard about his death."

"Both of the guys were trash-talking to him and demanding that Jesus prove Himself to them by performing some sort of miracle if God was with Him."

"I remember something like that."

I continued, "One of the guys came to his senses. He admitted that his life was not perfect and that he deserved his punishment for all the wrongs he had done. He also didn't want to gamble his life away. He probably thought to himself if Jesus was the Son of God this was his opportunity to say he was sorry."

"Go on."

"He also must have thought that Jesus was a King, because he asked that He would remember him when He entered his kingdom."

"Okay."

"A kingdom needs a king and Jesus must then be a king. Jesus, the king, then tells the man, 'Today you will be with me in paradise.'"

"In paradise," he replied, bowing his head.

I went on to say, "Your Creator, is he waiting for you on the other side of this life?"

"I don't know."

"Do you feel like you need to make changes in your life before you can ask your Creator to accept you and love you?"

"I guess."

"You aren't kept guessing with Jesus. He has always loved you. He will help you make the right choices and He will help you when you are tempted to do something that might get you back into jail."

"Why are you telling me all this stuff?"

"Because I know that you don't want to go back to jail but without Jesus to help you, it will be hard for you to stay free."

"You don't know how many times I have messed up in my life."

"No, I don't. But God does and He wants to forgive you right now if you'll let Him."

He sobbed, wiping his nose. "I don't want to go back to jail," he admitted.

"What's your name?"

"Fred."

"Can I pray for you, Fred?"

He nodded his head and I began to pray, "Lord, you know Fred. You know all his weaknesses and all his wrongs but You are willing to forgive him right now because You want to help him.

"Fred, do you acknowledge that you need Jesus in your life?"

"Yes."

"Do you acknowledge that you are a sinner by nature and that God wants to help you change your ways for the better?"

"I'm a sinner…forgive me, God. Help me to change."

"God, I release Fred into Your loving arms because I know that You deeply care for him. Help him to learn Your ways, and give him the strength to resist temptations that might land him into trouble. In Jesus' name, Amen."

"Amen." Fred stood up and shook my hand.

"I hope to see you soon," I said.

"You will," he replied, and walked towards the door.

Before he exited, I asked, "By the way, what did you serve time for recently in jail?"

"Armed robbery."

Staying calm, I inquired, "How long did you serve?"

"Was given a five-year sentence but I was out in three years."

"Go in peace." I replied.

He smiled. "I will."

Two weeks later I saw Fred walking across the street. He did not see me but I saw him. It was a reminder to keep praying for him.

chapter twenty-one

Other
Worries

I had other worries, too. The enormous stress the pizzeria was bringing into my life kept growing. Our restaurant kept taking financial losses. In the media, all we kept hearing about was reports of businesses making difficult decisions to downsize or to file for bankruptcy. We had had another setback when our restaurant got broken into the morning of Christmas Eve 2008, two weeks before Anna was born. While he didn't get much cash, he left behind extensive damage to our door.

Seeing that I was exhausted and frustrated running the struggling restaurant by myself, Trudy came back to work a month after Anna was born. We could not afford to hire a babysitter nor did we want one so Anna became part of our family business. Many of our wonderful customers came to see her. They couldn't wait to meet little Anna.

The restaurant problems escalated one evening when someone shot at our windows. I heard the faint shots although the people inside the restaurant were oblivious to the danger, not being able to hear what I heard over their loud conversation. I kept calm and walked out of the restaurant to see who was doing this, and if there was any damage. No one was in sight. It looked like someone from the apartment buildings across the street could have done this. Three of our windows had small entry points but the windows hadn't shattered. I thanked God that Trudy and Anna were not there that night. I decided to keep this a secret.

We were in so much debt because of the restaurant. Family and friends had loaned me money to start up the business, believing in my dream of running a successful restaurant. Trying to take control of the financial disaster that I was in, I refused to quit. When credit card applications arrived in our mail, I applied, believing maybe this was the solution to this mess. But the high interest rates were killing the pizzeria instead of helping it survive. No matter what I did, I couldn't keep the business afloat. Shady business people were trying to give me advice about how to cheat on taxes and to hide money but I was not going to take the easy way out. I was going to trust in God at all costs to get me out of the mess that I had gotten myself into.

I felt like I was a failure to my family and friends but somehow, I kept going on. The bank was not willing to help unless there was a co-signer involved. This was not an option. I began to feel abandoned by God.

I was tempted to drown my sorrows. I would stop at beer vendors. I wanted to get drunk but I knew this would destroy my new family. Often, I cried in my car, thinking about what would happen if I were to die before getting out of this financial mess. I was despondent at the thought of not leaving anything other than a pile of debt to my wife and daughter. By God's grace, I shook off the temptations of getting drunk and quit feeling sorry for myself. Each time I made it back home sober with a smile to face another day.

Trudy was losing faith and hope as well. Tough times challenge people's character and the basis of their faith. Trudy's prayer life was shaken but we knew there was more to life than the business. The more I struggled, the more opportunities I had to encourage others who were facing hardships like us.

One summer night, I went to throw out the garbage from the restaurant. As I approached the garbage bin, I heard what sounded like a pellet shot ricochet off the ground at my feet. Something punctured a window beside me. Knowing I was in danger, I sprinted to the safety of the restaurant, locked the door behind me and told Trudy to get behind the counter with Anna.

"What's going on?" Trudy asked fearfully.

"Someone just shot at me!"

"Are you okay? Anna started to cry as Trudy trembled.

"This is the second time this has happened. I can't stand being here anymore," I confessed.

"What do you mean, 'the second time'?"

"A few months ago. I never told you but it happened when you and Anna weren't here. I didn't want you to worry about me, but now I can't hide it."

"We have to call the police."

"They won't do anything!"

"What?"

"I'll go get the car and come back to get you and Anna!"

"This is crazy," Trudy replied, still shaking.

I quickly walked to my car that was in front of the restaurant, put it in reverse and parked it in front of the doorway. I got out of the car and helped Trudy and Anna get in. As we quickly drove away, Trudy insisted, "Billy, we have to call the cops!" Anna was crying in the back seat.

"Fine!" I replied.

She flipped her cell phone open to call 911. I couldn't believe how quickly the police showed up to meet us in a nearby parking lot where we explained to them what happened. The police told us that any type of shooting was a high priority call. It was then that I finally realized how bad the situation was.

The police followed us back to the restaurant. We showed them the pellet holes in our front windows from the shootings a few months earlier and where I had been when someone shot at me twenty minutes before we called for help. The police told us that a forensic unit would come the following day to get a better look at what happened because it was too dark for them to do a proper investigation.

That night as we drove home, Trudy was upset with me. I let her express her anger and frustration without arguing. She was right.

The restaurant had hit a new low. Not only had we been shot at but there was not enough money to pay our rent, our utilities, credit cards or suppliers. Our landlord was very patient with us and often got his rent late without complaining. But others were growing tired of my excuses for not being able to pay them on time. The credit card companies would not reduce our interest rates. Things were getting so bad that we were receiving phone calls at home, threatening to take us to court. A realtor got involved, trying to sell the business for us, but it was too late.

God was not changing this situation for me. Trudy and Anna kept me going but I didn't know what to do except to keep hoping that things would turn around somehow.

chapter twenty-two

Finding Billy

In the midst of all the chaos in my life, I decided to make another attempt to make contact with Ashley when she turned nineteen. Feeling I had nothing more to lose, I prayed for God to give me the words to touch her heart. I handwrote a one-page letter to her. Ashley was going to visit my parents the week of her birthday so I asked my mother to give her the letter and a small gift from me. A month later Ashley wanted to see me, saying she was willing to give me another chance. She also wanted to meet Anna and Trudy, so I brought them along.

We met for lunch at my parents' house. This meeting went a lot better. I got to hug her briefly and gave her a kiss on the cheek. It felt good to be that close to my daughter. It warmed my heart even though it only lasted a few seconds. I had waited fourteen years for that hug and kiss.

Ashley picked up Anna and noticed resemblances between them. "We have the same lips, chin and eyes," Ashley commented.

Trudy and Ashley got along easily. I tried hard to allow Ashley to lead in that visit. When all was over we agreed to do it again. I was pleasantly surprised that all went as well as it did.

After much counseling from business friends, I made the decision I felt was best for our family: Vasilly's Pizzeria would be no more. Facing my family and friends to tell them the business would be closed was difficult and shameful. By the end of November 2009, we had said our thanks and goodbyes to most of our wonderful customers.

God was not to blame. Feeling that I had passed a test by not going back into my old lifestyle was worth losing the business. I thank Him each day for bringing Trudy and Anna into my life. Our restaurant experience did not defeat my wife's prayer life. She held on, and now prays with a grateful heart.

We continue to live in Landmark, Manitoba, but now we rent the lower level of my in-laws' house. Anna has brought so much laughter and new energy for life into her grandparents' lives. I don't know how I'll ever make it up to them for all their love and sacrifices for us.

Hearing little Anna calling me, "Da-dee" every morning not only puts a smile on my face, it also puts life in perspective.

Having my two daughters meet and taking a picture with both of them is priceless.

Ashley and I finally went on a coffee date. Time has healed her heart and mine. It brought such great cheer to hear her tell what she envisions her future to be. We continue to work on restoring our relationship.

My cousin Pastor George has helped me immeasurably in my walk with Jesus. George's love and faith have challenged me to seek God's will in my life more intensely. We continue to meet when we can to encourage one another and to pray for each other.

God has been very loving and merciful towards me. He sent me to Pastor Clint Toews who mentors me and teaches me about the father-heart of God. Clint courageously challenges me never to let go of God's loving hand. That has helped to bring healing in many areas of my life.

I'm also grateful to Susan Danos, the friend who confronted me about my drinking at my friend's wedding. She stood up to me because she was not willing to see me compromise my life.

I have learned to appreciate things about my family that I didn't know before. After my parents came to Canada, they sent money each month to help support their parents in Greece. Grandma Eleni, my father's mother, left a legacy of love and nurturing in her village. She was the midwife, and she helped look after many of the children in her village. When my mother's stern father died, he left an envelope addressed to my mom. It was to be given to her when she next returned to visit her hometown. Inside was a check with all the money that my mother had sent to her parents, plus interest. My grandfather was a sweet man after all. Many people from his hometown who attended his funeral gave wonderful testimonies about Papou George helping them out financially when they were in great need. He truly was a remarkable man. I wish I could have had the chance to know him better. My mother's mother, Yiayia Eva, was diagnosed with Alzheimer's but she remembered her own father and Jesus to the end of her life.

Dad and I talk on a daily basis, whether in person or on the phone. He has also attended my church to support me when I have spoken. He tells me that he loves me lots, and I love him.

Mom's faith and love for God is something to marvel at. Both she and one of my sisters received long-awaited answers to prayer. My sister's answer came when I was baptized in March 2002. My mother's prayers were answered the first time I spoke at our church that same year. Mother could not stop crying. After the message, I asked her if everything was all right.

"When you were in prison I asked, 'God, why can't my boy be a priest and speak in church one day like his cousin George does? God heard that prayer,'" she continued. As we hugged, I could tell that her tears were happy ones.

God continues to heal and to restore our family. I had already apologized to two of my sisters for my failings, but my oldest sister felt left out.

I hadn't helped celebrate when the oldest of my sisters graduated from high school in 1991. Not long after, she had moved to Montreal to attend university there. (Our youngest sister joined our oldest sister in Montreal, then married, had two children and returned to Winnipeg.) In 2006, my oldest sister and her husband moved to Winnipeg and opened their

Italian restaurant just one month after we opened Vasilly's Pizzeria. I invited her to come to see the way we planned to renovate our restaurant. As we chatted about that, I took the opportunity to apologize for missing her high school graduation. She didn't say anything, so I continued. I admitted that I had been selfish. I had failed to give my sisters the love and protection they should have been able to expect from their oldest brother. When I asked for forgiveness, she responded with tears in her eyes. We hugged, and I gave her a kiss. Little did she know how much I had missed both her and my baby sister. That was why I had prayed that they would move back to Winnipeg.

I had to clear things up with my brother too. In 2007, when he helped us move from Winnipeg to Landmark, I had a chance. After we unloaded the five-ton truck he had borrowed, we returned it to Winnipeg. During the forty-five-minute ride, I thanked him for his help. Then, I shocked him with an apology. I confessed that I had failed him as an older brother by misleading him. He was silent. I saw tears in his eyes, but he didn't say anything. I didn't blame him. It must have been hard to think about all the deep pain I had caused.

When he dropped me off to pick up my vehicle, I thanked him again. The hurt still showed on his face.

Two years later, just before we closed our restaurant, My brother came to see me at work. He said he forgave me. Tears of relief flowed as we hugged. I asked why it had taken so long for him to forgive me. He had become a Christian a few months earlier. He admitted, "I wanted to hate you. You introduced me to cocaine and it nearly destroyed me." Then he went on, "I'm clean now, and I've realized it's wrong to hate you. You're released. I love you."

I had forgotten about the drugs, and I apologized again. I agreed when he said it was time we made a new start. I am so thankful for his love, and that he doesn't have to carry that hate anymore.

In 2011, we found out that Trudy was expecting again. When we went for our first ultrasound, the sonographer called Anna and I in.

The sonographer circled something on the video screen and said, "There he is."

"Did you say 'he'?" I asked.

Trudy smiled at me while holding my hand, and I looked up at the screen again. The sonographer found a few more different angles, proving it was a boy. I was stunned and shocked.

Anna said, "Look, I can see feet!"

We looked at the screen and she was right. I think the sonographer was even more surprised than we were at Anna's observation. "Very good!" The sonographer smiled at Anna.

That night I could not sleep I was so anxious and nervous. I was wondering how was I going to raise a son and prevent him from having the difficult trials I faced growing up. I took it up in prayer and started asking God to break the generational curses that have affected our family for so many years. I prayed the same prayer for Anna and for any future children that may come.

The next day we told Trudy's parents and later that evening we drove to Winnipeg so I could tell my parents. Trudy and Anna waited in the car. Dad was having supper and Mom was in the kitchen. I asked my father to come into the kitchen and he followed. "What is it, son?"

I smiled, "Last night we went and saw the baby on the ultrasound machine."

"Your mother told me. Everything is well, I heard."

"Yes…everything is well."

"How come you're smiling like that?"

"You're going to have your first Vassilopoulos grandson!"

"A boy! A boy!" Dad replied, jumping up and down like a little boy himself.

Mom quickly hugged me and congratulated me, kissing me on the cheek. Dad and I hugged and we started bouncing up and down as he kept kissing me. I nearly wept, thinking how far we've come. God has brought my father and me close together.

When I returned to the car where Trudy and Anna were waiting, my eyes were still misty, but I was grinning. Trudy knew that things had gone well and that I was emotional about telling my father the good news.

While we were courting and talking about our future, I had told Trudy that I would love to honor my father by naming our first son Andreas if that was all right with her. Trudy told me she liked that name. We wanted to honor our fathers by naming our son after both his grandpas.

Our son's due date was November 25, 2011. He decided to take his time and we had to wait until December 6, 2011 to meet Andreas Jacob. Half an hour after he was born, I phoned my father. Andreas was crying in the background.

"Is that my grandson?" Dad asked, his voice crackling.

"Yes, that's him."

"Put him on the phone, please."

"Okay…" I replied, and put the phone close to the baby's mouth.

After a few seconds, I went back to the phone only to hear my father crying with joy. "Did you hear him?" I asked.

"It was the most beautiful sound I have heard in a long time. Congratulate Trudy and give Anna a big kiss from me. Thank you for calling and letting me know that he's here and give him lots of kisses from me as well. I love you, son."

"I love you too, Dad."

Today, I'm proud of my father who continues to fight the terrible mental illness of bipolar disorder. I was once ignorant of his disease and suffering, but now I have a great deal of respect for what he is going through. Dad is the most beautiful man in the world to me. His courage and strength is something I marvel at. His honest love for his family is something I admire and appreciate. Though he fights the demons of his past, he is still the strongest man in the world to me. Simply put, Dad is my hero. When I visit him, I look forward to his kiss on my cheeks, even though I sometimes pretend that I want him to stop kissing me so much. God has redeemed my relationship with my father and has taught me that love and grace are gifts not to be taken advantage of. I encourage all men to give their fathers a second or, if needed, a ten-thousandth chance, for their own sake and healing.

I have learned that being a Christian doesn't make your life easier. It just makes it better. I have also learned that a life with adversity develops good character for those who choose not to give up. God must love my mother dearly, for He has answered another prayer for her. I'll be going to Bible College for four years, and I'm looking forward to earning a bachelor's degree in Pastoral Ministry. Once I was puzzled about the man with the fiery eyes I dreamed about. Now I have a new identity, for that same fire now lives in my heart and I will never stop following the fire from who it comes.

I now know the cleansing fire that transforms a person, and one of my dreams is to help bring transformation to an area where gangsters, teen prostitutes, crack houses, theft, murder and poverty continue to destroy lives.

Even though it was rough living there, I love the community where I grew up, and I want it to be a good place for families in the future. I suppose some might think I want to try to reform the neighborhood to make myself look good but that is not the reason.

I've found out who Billy really is. My reputation doesn't depend on who my parents are or what I've done. My reputation rests on the living God who loves me and sent His Son to be my Savior.

Dedicated to my Father

Son on Your Shoulders

I remember the top of your head
When you put me on your shoulders
I remember the smell of your clothes
When you walked down our street after a long
    day's work
I remember the way you said you loved me
With your smile and then with a kiss on my cheek
Daddy, what I didn't know was your childhood hurt
Daddy, what I didn't know was one day that this hurt
Would take you away from me and everyone close
    to you
You tried to drown your sorrow with alcohol
But you could not escape the tricks in your mind
You fight so hard and suffer much
I prayed for you and for God to touch
To touch your childhood heart
To free you from your pain and to tell you it was
    not your fault
Daddy…I remember the awful day we fought
I remember…I remember
Daddy, I remember the top of your head
When you put me on your shoulders
I remember the smell of your clothes

When you walked down our street after a long
    day's work

I remember the little puddle of blood on my bed-
    room floor

I remember the day the guards hauled me off and
    you wanted to hold me

I looked into your eyes and lost sight of that child-
    hood boy

I remember…I remember…

I remember the top of your head

You put me on your shoulders

I remember the smell of your clothes

When you walked down our street after a long
    day's work

Somehow God found me as I was drowning in my
    own sorrow

I remember crashing onto my bed

Closing my tired eyes and feeling the burning in
    my chest

I remember…Daddy…I remember

A hand grabbed my aching soul and said, 'This is
    not it!'

A year later I surrendered my old ways and thoughts

You seemed puzzled

Could Jesus really save my lost son?

I remember the top of your head

You put me on your shoulders

I remember the smell of your clothes

When you walked down our street after a long
  day's work
I remember looking into your childhood eyes
And seeing the scared little boy you tried to cover up
I remember the shaking of your frame
When I asked you to forgive me for all my wicked
  childhood ways
We both cried and hugged so tight
Our hearts were healed that night
I remember the top of your head now
Because I'm simply taller than you
Today I see the weight of the world on your shoul-
  ders
Today I love to smell your clothes when we hug
Today I know the fight you have and the long walk
  to recovery
Today, Daddy, I know that you have come home to
  my heart
Daddy, today I know…I know

Love your son,
Vasilios (Billy) Vassilopoulos

Also by the Author

In *Eyes Above the Water* Bill interviews survivors of attempted suicide, those bereaved by suicide loss, indigenous leaders, as well as people in the political, mental health, agricultural, educational, religious, and media sectors to find out "why is suicide still a problem in our world?" His real, raw, and respectful handling of a difficult subject brings hope and help to suffering families and communities. *Eyes Above the Water* is scheduled for release later in 2018.

CPSIA information can be obtained
at www.ICGtesting.com
Printed in the USA
BVHW04s0001250618
519716BV00005B/34/P

9 781486 615452